THE LIFE AND WORKS OF
MONET

73. Cl. Monet

THE LIFE AND WORKS OF
MONET

A DETAILED EXPLORATION OF THE ARTIST, HIS LIFE AND CONTEXT,
WITH 500 IMAGES THAT REPRESENT HIS ARTISTIC ACHIEVEMENTS

SUSIE HODGE

HERMES
HOUSE

This edition is published by Hermes House, an imprint of Anness Publishing Ltd, Hermes House, 88–89 Blackfriars Road, London SE1 8HA;
tel. 020 7401 2077; fax 020 7633 9499
www.hermeshouse.com;
www.annesspublishing.com

Anness Publishing has a new picture agency outlet for images for publishing, promotions or advertising. Please visit our website www.practicalpictures.com for more information.

Publisher: Joanna Lorenz
Project Editor: Anne Hildyard
Designer: Sarah Rock
Production Controller: Wendy Lawson
Indexer: Ann Barrett

ETHICAL TRADING POLICY

PUBLISHER'S NOTE

Although the information in this book is believed to be accurate and true at the time of going to press, neither the authors nor the publisher can accept any legal responsibility or liability for any errors or omissions.

PICTURE ACKNOWLEDGEMENTS

The publisher thanks the following picture libraries for the use of their pictures in this book. Every effort has been made to acknowledge the pictures properly.

l=left, r=right, t=top, b=bottom, bl=bottom left, br=bottom right, m=middle, tr=top right.

CONTENTS

INTRODUCTION

Monet is famously associated with Impressionist painting, with its emphasis on the changing qualities of light, bold colour and quick brushstrokes. Although his style evolved, his love of painting landscapes never wavered, and these works still have an enduring influence.

In 1874, when Claude Monet's painting *Impression, Sunrise* was first exhibited, critics and the public were outraged. The loose, sketchy painting went against all traditional art before it and critics lashed out immediately. "Wallpaper in its embryonic state is more finished than that seascape," mocked one respected painter. Yet within six years, the hostility had subsided and Impressionism, which had taken its name from Monet's painting, had won acceptance. It became one of the major art movements of the late 19th century, with an appeal that has endured into the 21st. Monet, often called 'the father of Impressionism', has come to epitomize the movement, with his light, bright canvases sporting sun-dappled waters and gardens, ephemeral effects of weather and atmosphere and his brilliant palette of colours.

AN ABUNDANT LEGACY

Over the course of his life, Monet produced more than 2,000 paintings and 500 drawings. Like all the artists he associated with, his development was individual, his focus and determination channelled and his output unstinting. Rejecting conventional training offered at long-established institutions, he mixed with the avant-garde of his day, rebelling against accepted methods of painting, enduring poverty and rejection and, in the traditional sense, suffering for his art. By the end of his 86 years, however, he was firmly established and accepted as one of the greatest and most popular artists of all time.

Monet's life was exceptionally full. He travelled extensively around parts of France and Europe and painted prolifically wherever he went, never tiring of interpreting what he saw. His inventiveness was boundless and his art was revolutionary at the time. Yet our familiarity with the millions of commercial reproductions – on trays, umbrellas, T-shirts, mouse mats and more, or the actual paintings hanging in galleries and museums around the world – has desensitized us to many of Monet's works. This is always a problem with a successful artist in our highly commercial world. It is only by studying his progression with fresh eyes, from his youthful experiments to his final epic paintings, along with some of the content of his 3,100 letters and contemporary social and political events, that we can begin to really comprehend the man and his work.

Below: View of Bordighera, Italy, *was painted by Monet in 1884. He described Bordighera as an "earthly paradise".*

Above: This photograph, taken c.1920, shows Monet on the Japanese bridge in his garden at Giverny.

SELF-DOUBT

From the start, Monet's paintings were always assured. They demonstrate his sensitivity to nature, his empathy with the changing seasons and times of day, his appreciation of the period, and his remarkable control of brush and paint. The conviction with which he handled his materials is apparent, yet letters he wrote to his family, friends and dealers are filled with modest anxiety about his work and his reverence of nature. The doubts and insecurities revealed in his letters are never apparent in his works. He remained resolute and energetic, striving day after day, year after year, not so much arrogant as persistent in his efforts, to improve and to recreate the ephemeral effects that he felt eluded him.

A MAN OF CONTRADICTION

While determined to resolve what he felt about his art with what he produced, Monet was frequently egotistical and demanding at home. Although it could be attributed to

Right: One of Monet's later paintings was Charing Cross Bridge, La Tamis, *1903. His early works, such as* Impression, Sunrise, *1872–73, show the same approach to light.*

'artistic temperament', he could be quite unbearable at times, particularly when he felt his work was not going according to plan. He was concerned about his reputation, his standing among the other Impressionists and the perception others had of his lifestyle. He enjoyed the finer things of life, such as good food, clothes and company and by the turn of the 20th century he lived as an English gentleman, having suits made to order of English wool and sitting down each morning to an English breakfast. He moved in cultivated circles

Above: This photograph, taken by Theodore Robinson in 1880, shows Claude Monet in his garden, which inspired many of his greatest paintings.

and conformed to accepted standards of the day, yet in his art he challenged convention and created motifs for his work from modern life.

By the time of his death, his works were renowned throughout the world and he had influenced a new generation of artists, shaping the direction of painting over the next century.

MONET, HIS LIFE AND TIMES

For over 40 years, Monet worked against the rigid conventions that were deeply embedded in French art. He grew up in a time when artists trained according to an inflexible formula, established since the Renaissance. Audiences expected to view images in a classical style rather than look at what seemed to be unfinished paintings. Despite constant criticism, his family's lack of support, and frequent financial distress, he remained faithful to his aims of capturing light and shade. To this end, he travelled around seeking new landscapes and subjects, and his household moved around with him.

Left: In the Woods at Giverny: Blanche Hoschedé at her Easel with Suzanne Hoschedé Reading, *1887. In later life, Monet experienced a happy family life. Here, he captures his stepdaughters in his garden.*

ARTISTIC
EVOLUTION

When he first saw them as a teenager in Le Havre, Monet had scoffed at Eugène Boudin's seascapes. When Boudin pointed out that Monet possessed all the natural attributes of the landscape artist – an instinctive affinity with nature, economy of line and a recognition of essential elements – it was a revelation that was to influence his work during his whole life. However, it took him years to be appreciated by the art establishment and the public.

Above: A detail from the painting Le Déjeuner sur L'Herbe, *1865–66. Left:* A Pathway in Monet's Garden, Giverny, *1902. At the end of the sun-dappled path is his house.*

GROWING UP

On 14 November 1840, in Paris, Oscar-Claude Monet was born. When the family moved to Le Havre, the sea views and changing weather were to later influence Monet's vision of nature. His first success at the age of 15 was selling caricatures of local people.

Oscar-Claude was baptized when he was six months old at the church of Notre-Dame-de-Lorette in Paris. Growing up, he was known as Oscar, but by the time he was 22, he had dropped Oscar and was using the name Claude instead. He grew up in a fairly musical environment, redolent with the sounds of his mother singing. Exactly what his father did for a living in Paris has never been established, but it is known that he did not earn much and had some financial difficulties.

THE MOVE TO LE HAVRE

In 1845 Monet's father, Claude-Adolphe Monet, moved with his wife, children and parents to the resort of Le Havre on the Normandy coast, where he joined his brother-in-law's wholesale grocery business. To help make ends meet, the Monet family also took boarders into their home.

When he was 11, Monet left his private primary school and entered the local community college just a short walk from his home. There he studied the usual subjects, including history, Latin, Greek, French, mathematics and art. Taught by Jean-François Ochard (1800–70), a former pupil of Napoleon's court painter Jacques-Louis David (1748–1825), art was Monet's favourite subject. Ochard taught traditional figure drawing by making his students copy plaster casts of famous statues, which was not to Monet's taste, although he quite enjoyed the process. His own choice of art is apparent in his school books, which are filled with doodles and caricatures of his teachers, as well as the boats and aspects of his local environment. Never one to conform, he did not enjoy school life and later said, "Even in my childhood, I could never be made to obey rules... The school always felt to me like a prison and I could never resign myself

Above: This albumen silver print shows Napoleon III on the Imperial Yacht at Le Havre in 1856. At the time, Monet was 16 and often sketched boats in the port.

to living there even for four hours a day." In contrast, he was happiest when he was outside by the sea. "When the sun was inviting, the sea was beautiful and it felt so good running along the cliff tops in the open air, or splashing about in the water."

REGENERATION AND DEATH

In June 1853, Baron Haussmann was named by Napoleon III as Prefect. His job was to redesign Paris, eliminating the disease-ridden, overcrowded slums. His ideas of regeneration were considered so positive and coherent that similar plans were adopted in all the great French cities, including Marseille, Lyon, Bordeaux, Montpellier, Rouen and Le Havre. In August 1857, Napoleon III and his wife, the Empress Eugénie, made an official visit to Le

Above: Monet exaggerated features, as in this pencil and gouache portrait of Black Woman Wearing a Headscarf, 1857.

Above: Dandy with a Cigar, *1857, is a typical example of one of Monet's caricatures, with overstated features and a typical dandy's paraphernalia.*

Havre to witness the redevelopment for themselves. New suburbs and docks were being built and street lighting spread throughout the city. Monet's sketchbooks at this time were filled with drawings of buildings that were later demolished.

At the same time, personal tragedy occurred. Monet's mother died on 28 January 1857 and, naturally enough, a cloud of depression pervaded the household. Monet left school that summer, probably without his Baccalauréat. Preoccupied with grief, his father did not have much time for him, but his father's half-sister, Monet's aunt Jeanne Lecadre began taking a close interest in her nephew. A childless widow, she took up painting and welcomed Monet into her home. She introduced him to her friend, the

Above: A Hunter and his Dog, c.*1858. Monet's reputation as a talented caricaturist soon spread around Le Havre. People made a point of walking by Gravier's shop window to see his new additions every Sunday.*

painter Amand Gautier (1825–94) and even in later years, Monet continued a lively correspondence with his aunt, sometimes consulting her on artistic matters.

Despite Adolphe's consternation, Jeanne Lecadre realized that her nephew would not join the family business. Instead of trying to make him conform, she encouraged his artistic aspirations – with reservations – and gave him a small allowance aiming to steer him toward a respectable artistic career. She had some knowledge and appreciation of progressive painting, so she did not expect him to conform too much, just to take steps to underpin his skills with some type of proper tuition.

CARICATURES

The caricatures that Monet had been drawing for fun in school became his first means of earning money. He often charged between 10 and 20 francs for his drawings of the citizens of Le Havre and he became something of a local celebrity. Signing them 'O. Monet', they were displayed in the window of Gravier, a local stationer, framer and ironmongery shop. Passers-by would gather and admire them, while Monet strolled by seemingly nonchalantly, but as he later admitted, "bursting with pride". By exaggerating certain identifiable features, Monet made humorous images out of what were really straightforward portraits. His swift observation of characteristics and his mature interpretations are an early indication of his accurate and intuitive responses.

EN PLEIN AIR

Some unconventional landscapes and seascapes, painted by Eugène Boudin (1824–98), were displayed above Monet's caricatures in Gravier's shop window. Gradually, Monet embraced this style of outdoor painting and acknowledged Boudin's influence.

Initially, Monet, in accord with the public, did not like Boudin's paintings. They were simple studies of nature, of the local environment, painted in the open air. With the arrogance of youth, 18-year-old Monet scorned 34-year-old Boudin's work, confident that he knew more about art than the painter. Rejecting Gravier's persistent advice to meet Boudin, Monet did not believe that Boudin could teach him anything. Eventually, however, they did meet and Monet was flattered to be told that he had a gift. Boudin encouraged Monet to join him on a painting expedition.

PORTABLE PAINT
Painting in oils out of doors was a relatively new idea in the late 1850s. It had been made possible in the

Above: The Beach at Trouville, *Eugène Boudin, 1867. Monet "was interested in Boudin's frank approach to painting..."*

preceding decade by the introduction of portable tin tubes of oil paint. Previously, painters had made their own paints by grinding and mixing dry pigment powders with linseed oil, but once ready-mixed paints were available in tubes, many artists began painting, rather than simply sketching, in the open air. Boudin was one of a growing number of landscape painters who insisted that painting in front of a subject was the only way to capture a true representation of a scene. He insisted that painting *en plein air* was more accurate than studio painting and was the method that Monet should be

Below: A Corner of the Studio, 1861, a still life featuring his painting materials, and showing his understanding of perspective.

FIRST HANDLING OF COLOUR

Before tube paints had been invented, an art student would initially spend a great deal of time practising with pencil and charcoal before moving on to paints and pastels several months later. Because of the way in which he worked, in front of his subject, painting very quickly on the spot, Boudin was keen to show Monet how to use both paints and pastels immediately and Monet relished applying thick, bright colours from his first open-air painting sessions.

Above: View from Rouelles, 1858. *This is believed to be Monet's first open-air landscape, painted when he was 17.*

using. He declared, "Three brushstrokes from nature are worth more than two days' studio work at the easel." Disinclined to believe him, Monet nevertheless bought a box of oil paints and accompanied Boudin to Rouelles, to the north-east of Le Havre.

For Monet, the expedition was almost a religious revelation. As he later recalled: "Boudin put up his easel and set to work…for me it was like the rending of a veil; I understood; I grasped what painting could be…my destiny as a painter opened up before me. If I have indeed become a painter, I owe it to Eugène Boudin…with infinite kindness he set about my education. Gradually my eyes were opened and I understood nature." Thirty years later, he wrote to Boudin, "I have not forgotten that it was you who first taught me to see and to understand."

MONET LEAVES FOR PARIS

Eager to expand his new techniques and to develop his skill even further, Monet announced to his father that he wanted to become a painter and so intended to go to Paris to study. Since this was completely alien to everything he knew, his father's first reaction was one of horror at such an impractical

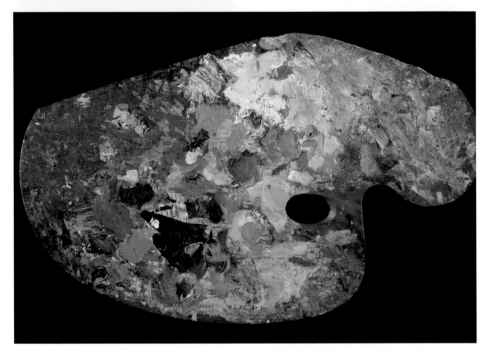

idea for a career, but with some gentle persuasion from Aunt Lecadre, Adolphe Monet soon acquiesced and submitted two applications for grants to Le Havre municipal authorities for his son to study art in Paris. Unfortunately, Monet's earlier success with caricatures went against him. The local authorities questioned whether fine art was the right career path for him when he had such a gift with caricatures. Both grants were refused, but, unaided by his father and with the blessing of his aunt, in April 1859, without waiting for the verdict of the second grant application, Monet took his savings and set off

Above: Encrusted with his paint, Monet's palette includes the colours lead white, chrome yellow, cadmium yellow, viridian green, emerald green, French ultramarine, cobalt blue, madder red and vermilion.

for Paris. His savings were quite considerable. From the sale of his caricatures, Monet had put aside 2,000 francs, more than an average working-class man would earn in a year. So the 19-year-old was confident of being able to exist on his savings for some time in Paris. He left in the spring in order to visit the Salon, which opened on 15 April.

THE ACADÉMIE SUISSE

On arrival in Paris, Monet went straight to the Salon, which opened on 15 April. There he saw the work of Constant Troyon and Charles-François Daubigny. Rather than join the studio of a recognized artist, Monet chose to enroll in the more informal Académie Suisse.

While in Paris, Monet wrote to Boudin to describe his reactions to the work of the painters of the Barbizon school, who exhibited in the Salon. Losing no time, he went to visit Boudin's former teacher and one of the artists who had impressed him, Constant Troyon (1810–65). Troyon admired the two still lifes he had taken with him and he advised Monet to copy works in the Louvre in the traditional manner. He also recommended that he should join the studio of Thomas Couture (1815–79), where Édouard Manet (1832–83) was also registered. Monet then visited Aunt Lecadre's friend, Amand Gautier and another artist whose paintings he admired, Charles Lhuillier (1824–98).

Above: Rue de la Bavolle, Honfleur, *1864. Monet has captured a charming street in Honfleur, bathed in sunlight.*

MONET'S FIRST ATELIER

Troyon's recommended path for Monet was met with approval by his father and aunt. Troyon suggested that Monet spend a couple of months working in Paris, then time in Le Havre studying landscape and seascapes, followed by a return to Paris to study in a traditional atelier for the winter. Adolphe Monet wanted his son to conform to accepted standards of the day and hopefully, become a successful painter in the process. To his dismay, however, his son did not conform. Instead of following this relatively academic path, he enrolled at the Académie Suisse, a private atelier run by Charles Suisse, a former model of Jacques-Louis David. Monet had intended to go to Couture's atelier as recommended by Troyon, but when Couture criticized the two still lifes that Troyon had praised, Monet was offended. After an argument, Couture refused to allow the young man to enter his establishment.

Among the students of the Académie Suisse were Delacroix, Richard Parkes Bonington (1802–28),

Corot (1796–1875) and Gustave Courbet (1819–77). For a small fee, Suisse offered his pupils the opportunity to work from live models rather than plaster casts and to follow their own style and choices of medium. There were no restrictions, no corrections and no examinations. Timing was also flexible. In summer the studio opened at six in the morning and the last class ran from seven to ten in the evening, so students could choose when to attend.

NEW FRIENDS

It was an exciting time to be in Paris. Between 1854 and 1858, Baron Haussmann began transforming the city by clearing a gigantic crossing in its centre. New boulevards were being

TRADITIONAL VERSUS RADICAL

The freedom with which students learned to create images at the Académie Suisse was instantly appealing to many avant-garde painters, especially landscape painters who wished to practise figure drawing without studying it excessively. In traditional studios, art students first learned to copy from engravings, then from plaster casts and finally from life models. Only after becoming a proficient draughtsman could a student start to use paint.

Right: Cattle going to Work, Troyon, *1855. At the Exposition Universelle, this was described as a "masterpiece". It was one of the sensations of the exhibition.*

constructed and it was at this period that it became called the city of light, with its new parks and boulevards and wide, well-lit streets. At the Brasserie des Martyrs, Monet financed his studies by drawing caricatures of the customers. There, and at the Académie Suisse, he made friends with those around him who had similar views about art. These included Corot, Courbet, Camille

Above: In terms of palette and handling, Farmyard in Normandy, c.1863, is unlike anything Monet was to do in later life.

Pissarro (1830–1903) and in 1861, Paul Cézanne (1839–1906). Pissarro had been at the Académie since 1855 and the two men instantly connected. Along with other students, Pissarro, Corot, Courbet and Cézanne's ideas concurred

Above: Hunting Trophies, 1862. This painting shows that Monet had the necessary skills to be a traditional artist.

with Boudin's in that they believed in painting directly from life and not trying to enhance nature. Monet said later that Pissarro was "tranquilly working in Corot's style. The model was excellent; I followed his example."

DISCOVERING DIFFERENT LIGHT

In spring 1861, Monet was selected to serve in the French army. At the time France had a system that determined who was called up for seven years of military service through the drawing of lots. In fact, the experience provided Monet with new ideas and influences.

The conscription law had been in place in France since 1855 and Monet unfortunately drew a low number, which meant he would be called up. His family offered to buy his discharge on the condition that he gave up his artistic ambitions, left Paris and joined the family grocery business in Le Havre, but nothing would deter Monet from his chosen path of being an artist. In fact, he was not particularly averse to a spell in the army and even found the idea of military life appealing. Attracted by the elegant uniform and the notion of a life of adventure, the paintings of the Orient he had admired at the Salon were also still fresh in his mind.

ALGERIA

Monet was drafted to the African Light Cavalry in June 1861 and was sent to Algeria. He later said that the bright light, intense colours and exotic culture affected the development of his painting style for the rest of his life. He described Algeria as "a splendid country with constant sunshine and hot, seductive colours, an eternally blue sky accentuated by the greens of palms and exotic plants." Although he discovered that military life was tedious, his sketching and painting made up for the monotony. To while away the time, he drew caricatures of others in his regiment and sent home small drawings of Algerian scenes. Describing his experiences later, he said, "I incessantly saw something new: in my moments of leisure I attempted to render what I saw. You cannot imagine to what extent I increased my knowledge and how much my vision gained thereby. I did not quite realize it at first. The impressions of light and colour that I received there were not to classify themselves until later, but they contained the germ of my future researches."

In 1862, he contracted typhoid and was sent home to France to convalesce. He spent his recuperation time drawing and painting with redoubled energy and after six months, Aunt Lecadre bought him out of the army. From this point, he began calling himself Claude as his comrades in Algeria had mocked the name Oscar.

Left: Portrait of Claude Monet in Uniform, *Lhuillier, 1861. A teacher at the École des Beaux-Arts, Lhuillier painted this dashing portrait of Monet.*

Right: The exotic palms, permanently blue sky and the bright sunlight of the desert in Algeria were to affect Monet all his life.

JONGKIND

That summer, Monet enthusiastically painted alone in and around Le Havre as Boudin was away painting in Honfleur and Trouville on the Normandy coast. While on one of his painting trips, he happened to meet an Englishman who introduced him to the Dutch painter, Johan Barthold Jongkind (1819–91), who was staying in Le Havre at the time. Monet was already an admirer of Jongkind's light, airy seascapes and subtle weather effects that he painted with loose, broadly brushed colours. Although Monet's family disapproved of Jongkind as he was an alcoholic and lived openly with his common-law wife, he was a kind and patient instructor. Monet later said that Jongkind "completed the training that I had already received from Boudin. He became from this moment, my true master, and it is to him that I owe the final development of my painter's eye."

Right: Seascape with Ponies on the Beach, *Jongkind, c.1870. Monet was inspired by Jongkind's handling and understanding of light.*

Below: The Joint of Meat, *1862–63. As a demonstration of his academic skill, Monet produced this picture for the Salon.*

TOULMOUCHE

When she bought Monet out of the army, one of Aunt Lecadre's stipulations was that he continued his artistic studies with a reputable painter in Paris. With this in mind, she arranged for him to be introduced to the painter Auguste Toulmouche (1829–90), who had won a medal at the Paris Salon in 1861, and who was married to a Lecadre cousin. In 1862, Monet gathered several of his recent landscape paintings and set off again for Paris. Toulmouche was impressed by Monet's natural talents and recommended that he join a reputable studio, preferably the one run by his own former tutor, Swiss-born Charles Gleyre (1806–74).

GLEYRE'S STUDIO

In the late autumn of 1862, Monet entered Gleyre's Academy and stayed for two years. At the Academy, he met Renoir, Sisley and Bazille, who became his fellow Impressionists, and joined them on expeditions to the forest of Fontainbleau, to paint open-air landscapes.

With new ideas about light, broken colour and quick brushstrokes, the foundations for Impressionism were just starting at this time of Monet's life.

MONET'S SECOND ATELIER
Gleyre's studio was one of many small ateliers run by artists. Remembering his own poverty as a student, Gleyre charged only 10 francs for models and for his teaching in the studio. This attracted many younger artists, including several of Monet's own age, among them Pierre-Auguste Renoir (1841–1919), Alfred Sisley (1839–99) and Frédéric Bazille (1841–70). Gleyre had been a successful artist in an idealized, highly finished style, but since 1852 had stopped exhibiting at the Salon. A shy and quiet man, he allowed his students freedom of expression and encouraged originality, although he made them all

Above: Portrait of Renoir, Bazille, *1867. Both the artist and sitter determined to achieve success through their painting.*

THE SALON
First introduced in the 17th century, the Salon was the official art exhibition of the Académie des Beaux-Arts in Paris. Held annually (and for a time, biannually) in the Palace of the Louvre until the end of the 19th century, it was the most important art exhibition in the world. Its original purpose was to display the work of final year students of the École des Beaux-Arts, but it soon extended to any artist who wanted to submit work for the selection committee. Work chosen for the Salon usually established artists' reputations. In 1863, the jury rejected more paintings than ever. Napoleon III agreed to display the rejected works in a separate exhibition in rooms in the Louvre and it became known as the Salon des Refusés.

begin with drawing – for six hours a day and six days a week – before they painted, which was one of the few ways in which he conformed to traditional methods of art teaching.

CLOSE FRIENDS
Even though their temperaments varied and they all came from different backgrounds, Monet, Renoir, Sisley and Bazille became good friends. Sisley was born in Paris to wealthy English parents, Bazille also came from a wealthy family and Renoir, like Monet, came from a working-class background and had earned his living as a porcelain painter for some time. Renoir recalled that Monet earned the nickname 'the dandy' at Gleyre's because, despite his lack of money, he wore lace-cuffed shirts and carried himself with an aristocratic air.

It was not long before the young men took themselves off on a painting expedition to Chailly-en-Bière near the

Above: Le Pavé de Chailly, 1865.
Monet became proficient at capturing the changes in the seasons.

Above right: Portrait of Auguste Renoir, *by Frédéric Bazille, 1867.*

forest of Fontainebleau to the south of Paris. Concerned that he was again rebelling against the conventional artistic teaching of Gleyre, Aunt Lecadre wrote to Monet, urging him to return to Paris. Whether it was the lure of the Salon, which was the official art exhibition in Paris, or the fear of his aunt's wrath, Monet was back there after a month.

PAINTING OUTDOORS

Monet, Bazille, Renoir and Sisley were not the only artists who painted open-air studies from nature. Boudin, Jongkind, Pissarro, Corot, Daubigny, Parkes Bonington and Courbet had all discovered the merits of painting landscapes as they saw them without adding any fashionable historical or mythological aspects. Earlier in the century, the English landscape painters, particularly John Constable (1776–1837) and J.M.W. Turner (1775–1851) had also produced numerous finished open-air studies.

Right: Spring Flowers, 1864. *Painted in careful detail, this still life retains a freshness and immediacy.*

PAINTERS OF RURAL LIFE

In 1864, Monet returned to Normandy with Frédéric Bazille, to take advantage of the special quality of the light in his open-air paintings. A row with his father put an end to this idyllic period and he returned to Paris to share a studio with Bazille.

At this time, the youthful Monet was painting prolifically and would spend whole days painting in the open air.

FONTAINEBLEAU

During 1863 and 1864 Monet periodically worked in and around the forest of Fontainebleau with Bazille, Renoir and Sisley. Their paintings were full of dappled light, bright colours and rapid brushstrokes and still at variance with acceptable styles of painting. Monet's handling and method acknowledged some conventional artistic features, but also introduced some original ideas of his own.

NORMANDY

In July 1864, he travelled to the banks of the Seine estuary in Honfleur. He wrote to Bazille, urging him to meet him there and Bazille soon joined him. They rented rooms and found an ideal spot for painting at a farm, where the farmer's wife brought them meals so they could paint all day without interruption. They got up at five each

morning and painted solidly until eight in the evening. At one time they crossed the estuary to Le Havre and Sainte-Adresse and painted there too. Bazille, who was also studying medicine, had to return to Paris to take some medical exams, but Monet remained at

Above: Terrace at Sainte-Adresse, *1867, with Honfleur at the horizon.*

Honfleur, painting landscapes, still lifes and flowers, which he described as "the best thing". Later that year, having failed his medical exams, Bazille decided to focus on a career in art and rejoined Monet. At different times throughout the summer, Boudin and Jongkind also painted with Monet in Le Havre, Rouen and Sainte-Adresse. Monet became captivated by the changes that occurred in nature over a period of weeks and in all weathers. At this time, he also concentrated on portraiture and figure painting, enjoying the exercise and outcome in contrast with his earlier caricatures.

That autumn he went to visit his family and spent time painting in and around Sainte-Adresse. It is not known exactly what triggered it, but he had a huge row with his father and was told

Left: A Cart on the Snowy Road at Honfleur, Snow, *1865, is typical of Monet's work during his time in Normandy.*

to "get out and not come back for a long time". The situation was dire as he was already struggling financially. In the end, Bazille paid for his return fare to Paris and he invited Monet to share his studio in the rue de Furstenberg. The situation of the studio in the centre of Paris was almost as inspiring to Monet as the country and sea had been and he set about painting several cityscapes. As well as a place where they could work freely, the studio became a meeting place for Pissarro, Courbet, Renoir and Sisley.

Above: Woman in the Forest, *1865, in which Monet emphasizes the dappled light and shadow through the trees.*

Below: The Improvised Ambulance, The Painter Wounded at Chailly-en-Bière, *1865, painted by his fellow artist, Bazille.*

MEETING CAMILLE

It was about this time that Monet first met Camille-Léonie Doncieux (1847–79). She was 18 and Monet was 25. She became his model in order to improve his figure painting and she soon became his girlfriend. At this time, Monet produced numerous portraits of Camille, in a variety of clothes and attitudes. Modern-day dress was generally considered unattractive and a poor focus for a worthwhile painting; historical scenes and costumes were deemed more acceptable. However, Monet depicted Camille and others in modern settings and contemporary clothing.

THE INFLUENCE OF MANET

The Salon des Refusés, which exhibited works rejected by the Salon, affected Monet profoundly, in particular a painting by Édouard Manet (1832–83). It was *Le Déjeuner sur l'Herbe*, which depicts a naked woman sitting on the ground with two fully clothed men.

This period in Monet's work was just prior to his adoption of the characteristic features of his Impressionist style.

LE DÉJEUNER SUR L'HERBE

Manet's painting shocked and horrified the critics. It alluded to mythological and rural works by Titian (c.1487–1576) and Giorgione (c.1476–1510) and criticized the art world's love of highly idealized paintings in a precise, smooth and realistic style, but it also demonstrated an artist's independence.

The scandal of a naked woman casually lunching with two fully dressed men was considered offensive and controversial, but also, the background lacked depth, the lighting and application of paint was inconsistent and the entire work seemed unfinished and unnatural. Taking ideas from popular Japanese prints, Manet had flattened areas of his painting, accentuating the position of each element and making the brushmarks apparent rather than trying to recreate a photographic likeness of the scene.

INSPIRATION

Because of the similarity of their names, when Monet's work was exhibited at the Salon of 1865, Manet was mistakenly praised. Instead of being flattered, Manet was incensed. "Who is this Monet?" he asked anyone who would listen. "He appears to have appropriated my name with a view to benefiting from the stir that is being made about me." On another occasion he was heard to declare, "Who is this urchin with his despicable pastiches of my painting?" Monet felt far more positively inclined toward Manet's work. Two years previously, Monet had described his reaction to Manet's *Le Déjeuner sur l'Herbe* as a "revelation". In 1865 he decided to paint his own version, telling Bazille that he was planning on executing an immense composition, also called *Le Déjeuner sur l'Herbe* out of respect for Manet's work.

Unlike Manet's painting, Monet's composition was going to include a group of fully dressed people in the countryside picnicking, and in more natural attitudes than Manet's figures. The following spring, he returned to Chailly-en-Bière and began sketches for the background of this massive painting, planned for a canvas of about 4 x 6m (12 x 22ft). He became absorbed in the project and at one point, wrote to Bazille: "I no longer think of anything but my picture and believe I shall go mad if it doesn't work." Later that summer, he wrote to Bazille again: "I would like your opinion on the choice of landscape for my figures," and even later, "You must come and pose for some of the figures. If you don't, the picture will be a failure."

Left: The Promenaders, or Bazille and Camille, *1865. Sunlight in Fountainebleau forest highlights and defines their clothes.*

PAINTING IN THE STUDIO

For the first time since he had become a painter, Monet spent most of his time painting this canvas in a studio. The canvas was so large that it could not be painted out of doors, so he gathered material for the background by making sketches on the spot. His absorption kept him apart from his friends and that summer, Bazille spent most of the time away from Monet. In the end, he did not complete his *Déjeuner* but his next paintings of figures outdoors were filled with his immediate impressions of light and the surrounding landscape.

Above: Déjeuner sur L'Herbe, Chailly, *1865 (left panel). This work was to boost his career, but it was uncompleted.*

Above: Déjeuner sur l'Herbe, Chailly, *1865 (central panel). Monet painted the actual canvas in a studio.*

TWO-WAY INFLUENCE

Monet made no secret of his admiration of Manet's flat tones and unblended colours. Manet's scenes of modern life, with Parisian figures, were revelatory to the younger artist and his interest soon moved to scenes of contemporary life, inspired by Manet. Manet acknowledged the influence of Velázquez (1599–1660), but he later abandoned the dark colours inspired by the Spanish artist. Despite his early resentment, he became increasingly influenced by Monet and began using a lighter, fresher palette.

Left: Le Déjeuner sur l'Herbe, Manet, *1863. The attitude of the men, ignoring the naked woman, shocked the viewers.*

SUCCESS AT THE SALON

Woman in a Green Dress, 1866, showing his future wife, Camille Doncieux, was well received at the Salon. Spurred on by his triumph, he began elaborate preparations to paint his next entry for the Salon, *Woman in a Garden, 1867.*

Monet's ambition to get recognition for his work at the Salon was finally achieved with his portrait of Camille.

LIFE-SIZE CANVAS

Monet enjoyed painting modern figures acting naturally in garden settings, but he did not take pleasure in painting the entire canvas indoors and tried to do much of it outside. Still, before he had completely turned his back on painting indoors, he painted a life-size canvas of Camille. Amazingly, considering how long he had spent on *Déjeuner,* his previous work, *Woman in a Green Dress*

Below: Woman in a Green Dress, *1866, was painted with the aim of succeeding at the Salon.*

was completed in four days and painted specifically for submission to the Salon of 1866. He submitted two paintings and both were accepted, a considerable achievement for such an unknown artist. The painting of Camille was highly praised and described in the magazine *L'Artiste,* as "the Parisian queen, the triumphant woman".

SÈVRES AND SAINTE-ADRESSE

After his success with *Woman in a Green Dress,* Monet was determined to produce another work featuring figures in a landscape. He left Paris for Sèvres in the south-western suburbs of Paris, writing to Gautier from there: "I am happier than ever…I am working a lot and my courage is higher than

ever. My success at the Salon secured me several picture sales." He also told friends that on finding the perfect location for a new painting, *Woman in a Garden,* he rented a house and dug a trench in the garden. Through a network of pulleys, he managed to raise and lower his enormous canvas and so paint any part of it on the spot. Although this is not out of the bounds of reality considering Monet's personality, it has never been verified. Essentially, he was making sure that everyone knew he was producing a *plein air* painting.

Even though he added finishing touches to it in a studio in Honfleur, most of it does seem to have been executed outside. The finished painting

OLD AND NEW

The essential distinction between *Woman in a Green Dress* and works by his friends is the way in which Monet mixes old and new. Once again, convention and innovation are mixed, by portraying a modern woman in fashionable clothes, in the intense, dark tones of traditional portraiture. She is neither a modest saint, nor a haughty monarch, but a contemporary woman. While his friends were all for a fresh approach, they had never gone this far: Monet painted in the new loose manner, often mixing traditional and modern features. This style became one of the main focuses of Monet's work for the next several years. The publicity that the painting generated allowed Monet to sell several more of his paintings, and two years later the editor of *L'Artiste,* Arsène Houssaye (1815–96) bought *Woman in a Green Dress* for 800 francs.

is again a picture of modern life set in a natural landscape. With vigorous brushstrokes and vibrant colours, dappled sunlight creates patterns on the fashionable gowns worn by the women, three of whom were posed by Camille.

Above left: A Jar of Peaches, *1866. As with most of his still lifes, Monet painted this with small brushes and great detail.*

Above: Jeanne-Marguerite Lecadre in the Garden, *1867. The woman in white is a cousin of Monet's.*

ADDITION TO THE FAMILY

Earlier in 1867, Monet told his father that Camille was expecting his child. Adolphe Monet insisted that his son should leave Camille if he wanted to benefit from his family's generosity. That summer, Monet appeared to obey his father, leaving Camille in Paris and moving back with his aunt, where he painted another outdoor scene featuring figures, *Terrace at Sainte-Adresse*. Without their knowledge, he had told Camille to return to her parents and he would send her money when he could. On 8 August 1867, she gave birth to a son, Jean. Monet was delighted. In a letter asking Bazille to be the baby's godfather, he wrote: "A fat and beautiful boy….It pains me to think that his mother has nothing to eat."

Right: Flowering Garden at Sainte-Adresse, *c.1866. In this picture, horizontal layers of colour are balanced by vertical lines.*

MIXED FORTUNES

Although Monet was commissioned to paint a portrait, and had received praise for his work, it was not enough and he was feeling the effects of poverty. In 1869, Renoir came to his aid, taking Monet to paint at the resort of La Grenouillère, near Bougival.

Despite praise for *Woman in a Garden*, the painting was not accepted for the 1867 Salon. Instead, Bazille bought it for 2,500 francs the following year.

In that year, 1868, Monet had one painting accepted for the Salon and showed five paintings at the *International Maritime Exhibition* in

Left: Portrait of Claude Monet, *Carolus-Duran, (1837–1917), 1867. The artist was the future teacher of John Sergeant.*

Le Havre. The exhibition jury panel included his old art teacher, Ochard, and Monet was awarded a silver medal.

LOUIS-JOACHIM GAUDIBERT

By that time, Monet, Camille and Jean were living together and Monet had registered Jean as his son, still without marrying Camille. His family continued to refuse to receive Camille and the baby, and Adolphe Monet completely withdrew any financial support. In August, Monet was commissioned by Louis-Joachim Gaudibert, a businessman from Le Havre, to paint a portrait of his wife. Both Gaudibert and his wife were delighted with the portrait, although other members of their family did not receive it well since he had curiously painted her turning away, almost from the back. Although he earned money

Above: Quai du Louvre, Paris, *1867. In spring 1867, Monet painted views of Paris. Here, he uses a light palette and touch.*

from the commission, the criticism upset Monet. He wrote to Bazille many times, lamenting his situation. "My painting isn't working at all…I no longer expect fame….On top of it all, there is still no money." Despite this gloominess, at the end of the year, Monet took Camille and Jean to live in Étretat, a seaside village near Fécamp on the English Channel. He soon recovered his old enthusiasm. "I am going into the country, which is so lovely now that I almost like it better in winter than in summer," he wrote to Bazille.

MEETING MANET

During the 19th century, cafés served as places for working men to eat a midday meal or to drink and discuss issues of the day in the evenings. When Monet returned to Paris in 1869 he occasionally frequented the Café Guerbois in the Batignolles quarter, which had become the meeting place of artists and writers. Manet was usually there and in debate with Zola, Bazille, Edgar Degas (1834–1917), Renoir and Sisley and sometimes Cézanne and Pissarro joined them. At last, Monet and Manet were introduced.

LA GRENOUILLÈRE

At the end of the year, Aunt Lecadre cut off any remaining allowance because of his relationship with Camille. On top of that, the work he produced in Étretat was rejected from the Salon of 1869. His situation was desperate and he moved again with his young family to Saint-Michel near Bougival. He wrote to Bazille, "No bread, no fire in the kitchen, no light for the last eight days." This time, Renoir came to his assistance. He brought bread to Monet and Camille and talked Monet into accompanying him on painting trips to the swimming resort and floating café on the Seine near Bougival, called La Grenouillère.

FIRST HANDLING OF COLOUR

The paintings Monet and Renoir produced at La Grenouillère were precursors of the Impressionist style and showed the radically new painting style that they were developing. They were determined to express the atmosphere of the place. For the first time, Monet captured fleeting moments by painting light effects. Previously, he had painted his subjects bathed in light. In the paintings he produced with Renoir during the summer of 1869, his theme was light. By quickly applying colour in broad, impasto brushmarks, he depicted a spontaneous impression of the scene. This is particularly apparent in his portrayal of the river, which is made up of slabs of broken colour.

Above: Portrait of Madame Louis-Joachim Gaudibert, *1868. The unusual position of the model was totally unconventional.*

Below: La Grenouillère, *1869. This was one of the most popular Sunday destinations for workers seeking relaxation.*

MEETING WITH THE DEALERS

Gaudibert continued buying work from Monet until his death in 1870, but with his few purchases, he could not keep Monet and his family above the breadline. However, a new form of help materialized in the form of an introduction to an art dealer.

Monet's lack of success at several Salons had an adverse effect on his income, and the draining away of his finances continued to be a major problem. In June 1869 he wrote in desperation to Houssaye, who was the editor of *L'Artiste*, asking if he would like to buy some of his paintings "before they are taken by the bailiffs".

In the autumn of 1869, Renoir returned to Paris and the painting expeditions to La Grenouillère ended. Monet went to Paris sporadically to meet possible buyers of his work or to catch up with friends at the Café Guerbois.

Monet also modelled for a couple of paintings by Bazille and another of his friends, Henri Fantin-Latour (1836–1904) and occasionally travelled to various locations to paint, but spent most of his time with his young family. That winter was particularly cold but Monet worked determinedly around the village of Saint-Michel. Sometimes he went to visit and work with the painter Pissarro, who lived nearby.

DAUBIGNY'S INFLUENCE

Since his first visit to the Salon of 1859, Monet had admired the work of Daubigny. He even possessed a painting by him, which he had found in Aunt Lecadre's studio in 1860. Daubigny was the son of a classical landscape painter who had first painted near Fontainebleau in 1834 and had his first success in the Salon in 1837. By 1859 he had been awarded three First Class medals, was commissioned to decorate the government office in the Louvre and was made a Knight of the Legion of Honour. In 1857 he had begun working from a floating studio boat, from which he painted views along the Seine, Marne and Oise rivers under varying atmospheric effects.

Monet often acknowledged his admiration of Daubigny and had made his acquaintance through other artists he mixed with. In 1870, Daubigny, who was often included as part of the Salon jury, joined Corot and Jean-François Millet (1814–75) in trying to obtain acceptance for Monet's submissions. When their views were disregarded,

ART DEALERS

The 19th century saw the emergence of a new career in the art world. Unlike patrons who bought art for themselves, art dealers bought art directly from artists and sold it on, earning a percentage each time. By 1861 there were more than 100 art dealers in Paris. Most displayed the art they had bought in commercial galleries, which began opening in various European cities during the mid-19th century. Rather than dealing directly with the artist, buyers could now liaise with dealers who might have a range of different artists' work. It was also often easier to transact with dealers than with artists. Dealers were open-minded about art and bought unconventional work. They also offered a range of useful services for artists, including financial help and the organization of art exhibitions.

Above: Bathers at La Grenouillère, *1869. Monet applied broad areas of colour for the reflections, boats and bathers.*

Left: La Grenouillère, Renoir, *1869. 'The frog pond' was located on a bend of the Seine. The effects of light on water particularly fascinated Monet and Renoir.*

Corot and Daubigny were furious and resigned from the jury. Some months later, Daubigny was to assist Monet in another way, when he introduced him to his art dealer, Paul Durand-Ruel.

This was to prove a productive meeting, for Paul Durand-Ruel (1831–1922), went on to buy many of Monet's paintings. He was one of the

Below: The Banks of the Oise, Morning, *Daubigny, 1866. The lack of finish in his landscapes attracted Monet to his work.*

first modern art dealers who supported his painters in many ways other than simply purchasing their work. His father had inherited a stationery shop and had digressed into art dealing by chance. In 1865, Paul inherited the business. He became known for buying works by avant-garde artists, including Eugène Delacroix (1798–1863), Corot, Daubigny and Courbet and he often reserved paintings from the Salon before it opened. He arranged art auctions and exhibitions and

Above: Stormy Sea at Étretat, *c.1868–69. Fascinated by storms and changes in the seasons, Étretat gave Monet plenty of scope.*

occasionally financed artists if they were experiencing hardship. In 1869, in partnership with another art dealer, Durand-Ruel founded the short-lived magazine *La Revue Internationale de l'Art et de la Curiosité,* which was intended to make people understand what many modern artists were attempting to achieve.

MARRIAGE

In 1870, Monet was married, and in February of that year, he painted in Bougival, on the Seine, with Renoir. Both were still struggling financially and they calculated that views of increasingly fashionable Bougival would appeal to Parisians.

On 28 June 1870, in a modest ceremony, Monet married Camille Doncieux at the town hall of the eighth arrondissement in Paris. Courbet was one of their witnesses. It is not clear why Monet married Camille then, after four years of living together intermittently. There was no big dowry from her parents and the marriage did not make much difference to his family's attitude – they still disapproved of the union. The small sum he was paid by Monsieur Doncieux was spent on canvases and other art supplies.

TROUVILLE

Soon after the wedding, Monet took Camille and Jean to Trouville on the Normandy coast, across the Seine estuary from Le Havre, a short distance from Honfleur. They stayed at the Hotel Tivoli. Trouville looked out on to the English Channel and featured a long stretch of sandy beach, which attracted many holidaymakers from both sides of the Channel. Since the

1850s, in common with so many areas of natural beauty, improvements in transport and working conditions meant that Trouville was becoming more popular. By 1870, several large hotels had been built along the new promenade that hugged the seafront

Above: The Magpie, 1869. *Using blue-grey, yellows, lilac and apricot, this work shows Monet's dazzling effects of light.*

and a casino, cafés, restaurants and souvenir shops had sprung up to appeal to visitors.

Monet painted nine pictures at Trouville that summer. He set up his easel either on the seafront terrace or on the beach and painted the carefree society enjoying their recreation. Highlighting his development, most juxtapose light and dark tones, with slabs of freshly coloured paint, reflecting the immediacy of his *plein air* method. It is possible that he intended to use these paintings as the basis for a large-scale picture of people at leisure, following on from Boudin's paintings of the seaside. Instead of concentrating on the sea, however, as Boudin had done, Monet focused on the beach and buildings. Several grains of sand are embedded in the paint of many of

Left: Camille on the Beach at Trouville, 1870. *In this study of sea and sand, Camille sits, holding a parasol.*

MARRIAGE 33

WAR AND MILITARY SERVICE

After a long period of discord that had started with the Napoleonic Wars, and recent diplomatic incidents, Napoleon declared war on Prussia. Bismarck used the resulting crisis as a means of unifying the German states. Within days, the efficient and organized Prussian army was on the march toward France.

There was a problem on Monet and Camille's wedding day. Unable to provide official documentation of his military service in Algeria, Monet had allowed himself to be accountable and likely to be called up to fight in the war. Later that summer, when the Franco-Prussian War was declared, although he could declare his marriage as a reason for exemption, without evidence of previous service, there was still a chance that he might be conscripted once more.

Right: The Hotel des Roches Noires at Trouville, *1870. In the summer season, Monet painted in light bright colours.*

these Trouville works, as evidence that he painted them on site. One of Monet's paintings from this time was a confident study of Camille on the beach at Trouville, characterized by broad, strong brushstrokes.

AUNT LECADRE

A few days after Monet's marriage to Camille, on 7 July, his Aunt Lecadre died at Sainte-Adresse. She was 80 years old and, against the rest of her family, had continued to believe in her nephew's talents. Two other nephews signed her death certificate. They possibly resented the allowance she had given their cousin. After her death, Monet had no one in his family who believed he was following the right path.

Right: The Bridge at Bougival, *1869. With financial troubles lingering, Monet painted at Bougival with Renoir.*

MONET IN LONDON

The Franco-Prussian war, 1870–71, was a personal tragedy for Monet; Renoir was called up and his friend Bazille was killed in action. Monet took refuge in London, with others in the artistic fraternity. This period was, however, a productive one for Monet.

By some official error, there was no documentation of Monet serving his country in Algiers, so the chance of being conscripted again was a risk for him.

FLEEING FROM FRANCE

To avoid the possibility of military service and to escape the horrors of his country, Monet left France for London with Camille and Jean in September, 1870, just before the Siege of Paris. During his stay, he produced about six paintings in all. These were views of Hyde Park, Green Park, the Thames and a portrait of Camille. His stay in London was fruitful in other ways, too. Several other compatriots had fled to England to escape the war, including Boudin, Daubigny, Durand-Ruel and from December, Pissarro.

THE SIEGE OF PARIS AND THE COMMUNE

Monet's decision to leave Paris proved to be a good one. After suffering crushing defeats by the Prussians, Napoleon III surrendered in September 1870 and was captured. A government of National Defence was formed, but the Prussians blockaded Paris. Disease and starvation spread, and in January 1871 Paris surrendered. Wilhelm I, the Prussian king, was crowned Emperor of Germany at Versailles. A French national assembly chose the first president of the Third Republic, who demanded rents from Parisians and ceased paying the National Guards. In March, Parisians broke out in revolt and organized a revolutionary government called the Commune of Paris. A civil war ensued between the Commune and the troops of the Versailles government.

A BENEFICIAL INTRODUCTION

In London in 1870, Monet's introduction to Durand-Ruel was a defining moment. For over 30 years, Durand-Ruel became Monet's main means of selling work. "Without him," Monet declared in later life, "We would have died of hunger…we owe him everything." In December 1870, Durand-Ruel opened a new gallery in London and included one of Monet's canvases for the inaugural exhibition, which he called 'The Society of French Artists'. Monet also had a few paintings accepted for a

Top: The Port of London, *1871. This shows the Pool of London; the Customs House and London Bridge are behind.*

Above: The Thames below Westminster, *1871. Another view of London that showed Monet's mastery of composition.*

Above: Hyde Park, *1871. Monet, Camille and Jean stayed in London for nine months from 1870 to 1871.*

major international exhibition held at the South Kensington Museum in May 1871. Although his paintings did not sell, valuable contacts had been made.

ENGLISH LANDSCAPE

Together, Monet and Pissarro visited the London museums and galleries, seeing at first hand the works of the English landscapists who had painted the countryside and seascapes since the 18th century. The Frenchmen were extremely enthusiastic about the works of Constable and Turner. Constable had won a gold medal at the Salon in 1824, but since then had not been represented in France and no works by Turner had ever been displayed there, so neither Monet nor Pissarro had seen their work before. Claiming that painting was only another word for feeling, Constable had studied the incessantly changing appearance of nature, painting out of doors with lively, sketchy brushwork. Turner captured ephemeral effects of natural phenomena and surroundings, applying paint in a free, uninhibited manner and using

Above: The Scarlet Sunset, *Turner, c.1830–40, has the reflective quality that Monet later experimented with.*

colour and brush direction to express what he saw. Monet said admiringly that he and Pissarro had been "vividly impressed by the Turners in the National Gallery." He also referred directly to Turner's *Frosty Morning*, saying that he had "painted it with his eyes wide open."

In later life, Monet was ambiguous about Turner and said: "At one time I greatly liked Turner, but today I like him much less – he did not draw enough with colour and he used too much of it. I have studied him closely." It is likely that Monet also visited James McNeill Whistler (1834–1903), while in London, following earlier meetings in the Café Guerbois.

DUTCH INTERLUDE

As soon as they heard of the fall of the Commune, the Monet family left England in 1871. Not wanting to return to the volatile situation in France, Monet took Camille and Jean on a detour. With its expanses of water and changeable skies, Holland seemed the ideal place.

Monet travelled to Holland in May 1871. Daubigny had moved to Holland after London and recommended the town of Zaandam, near Amsterdam to Monet for its atmosphere and light conditions. The Monet family stayed there for four months.

ZAANDAM

In contrast with London, Monet was very productive in Holland and painted at least 24 canvases in Zaandam, so his sojourn there proved to be inspiring for him artistically and produced a slight improvement in his fortunes.

The scenery was calm and picturesque, with tall, leafy trees and a network of flowing canals. The gently rippling water reflected the sky, bridges, windmills, trees and buildings, which was a perfect mixture of elements for Monet at the time. He probably also welcomed the quietness after all the events – both personal and political – of the past year. Financially, things were slightly improved. Early in 1871, he had

Above: Zaandam, 1871. In Zaandam, Monet painted water subjects, using a brighter palette and sketchier brushwork than the 17th-century Dutch masters he had viewed in Amsterdam.

received news of his father's death at Sainte-Adresse, which meant he was now to have a small inheritance – not much as his father had very recently married his mistress, which diminished Monet's allowance. Camille began giving French lessons to the daughters of wealthy citizens of Zaandam and she also received a small inherited annuity. At the same time, Monet began receiving his first earnings from Durand-Ruel's sales of his work. That summer, he wrote to Pissarro: "We crossed virtually all of Holland and there is no doubt that what I saw of it is more beautiful than people say. Zaandam is particularly charming and there is enough subject matter here to last a painter a lifetime....The Dutch seem very likeable and hospitable."

DUTCH LANDSCAPE

The influence of 17th-century Dutch landscape art on certain French painters was apparent in the paintings that were produced throughout the 19th century. The Dutch landscapists of that time composed their pictures with low horizons and stark contrasts of dark against light. French Romantics, such as Delacroix, had acknowledged openly their warm admiration of Dutch art, particularly the works of artists Salomon von Ruysdael (c.1600–70) and Meindert Hobbema (1638–1709). Other painters that Monet admired and who gave him inspiration, were Corot, Troyon and Daubigny. They copied the works of well-known Dutch landscapists in the Louvre; these artists became known collectively as the Barbizon school.

Right: Garden House on the Zaan, Zaandam, 1871. Monet seems to have found peace and tranquillity in Zaandam.

He immersed himself in painting the houses, boats, mills, quays and canals and especially the reflections on the water and the changing skies. Toward the end of June, he wrote again to Pissarro, "I am starting to work feverishly and have hardly any time to spare." His paintings from this period are light, airy and sketchy, showing some acknowledgement of 17th-century Dutch landscapists that he saw when he visited Amsterdam's museums.

RETURN TO FRANCE
In the autumn of 1871, Monet returned to Paris. He was saddened to witness the damage caused by the Prussian siege. He and Camille stayed in the Hôtel de Londres, in front of the Gare Saint-Lazare. He had use of Gautier's studio and took up occupancy there immediately. He had several things to attend to, including retrieving the paintings he had left in the homes of Pissarro and Bazille while he was in exile for the duration of the war. It was distressing to organize the return of the paintings that Bazille had put into safe-keeping, knowing that he would never enjoy his friend's companionship again.

Below: Mills on the Zaan upriver from Zaandam, 1871. Monet could relax in Zaandam as his sketchbook studies show.

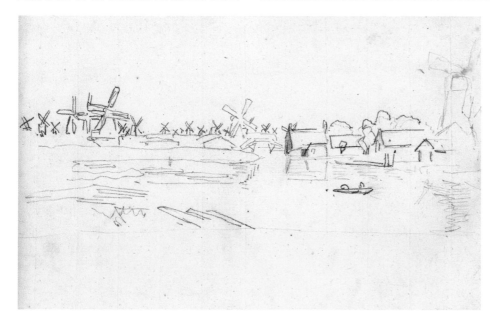

Above: Zaandam, 1871. For Monet, painting landscape epitomized his freedom of self-expression.

Boudin, Renoir and Pissarro often visited Gautier's studio as Monet worked and he set to work at once, completing the paintings from Zaandam in order to sell them. He met up with Durand-Ruel and with the art dealer Latouche, who had exhibited his work before the war. Durand-Ruel was in mourning following his wife's death, but Latouche bought one of Monet's Dutch landscapes. Boudin was particularly enthusiastic about the 20 canvases that Monet brought back from Holland.

IMPRESSION, SUNRISE

Through some influential friends who owned property there, Manet arranged for the Monet family to rent a house in Argenteuil in the suburbs of Paris. Some of the best and most famous Impressionist works were created there.

Situated to the north-west of Paris, Argenteuil was a growing industrial town built on a hill, which extended to the edge of the right bank of the Seine. At the junction of the northern and western railway networks, it was linked by a 30-minute train service to the Gare Saint-Lazare. Two bridges crossed the Seine nearby; one was a road and the other a railway line.

INSPIRATION IN ARGENTEUIL

With his proclivity for juxtaposing natural and manufactured objects in his pictures, features he noticed in Argenteuil gave Monet plenty of scope. Concrete, cast iron, brick and wood were not usually included in landscape paintings, but Monet frequently made a point of doing this. Farther down the river was a floating shed where rowing-boats could be hired, on the left bank was an area where walkers passed through tall poplars and in the town itself were factories, houses, gardens and orchards. Each gave Monet

Above: Impression, Sunrise, *1872. This painting of Le Havre shows the sun rising over the misty harbour, shrouding the commercial and industrial boats and reflecting red and orange on the water.*

possibilities for paintings. After a house warming party in January 1872, Monet's energy and enthusiasm could not be suppressed. Sisley was one of his first guests there and together, they painted the local area. Over the next few months, Monet painted the local environment, his friends and family, and his garden and explored different ways of representing figures in the landscape as he had done at the start of his career.

EXHIBITION IN ROUEN

Monet's fervour overflowed. His brother Léon most likely suggested that he submitted work for an exhibition in Rouen in March 1872. Léon had bought

Left: View of Mount Fuji from Satta Point in the Suruga Bay, *Hiroshige, woodcut published posthumously in 1859. This is one of 36 woodcuts of Mount Fuji seen from various viewpoints in different seasons. Monet was greatly influenced by Japanese art.*

one of his brother's Zaandam paintings and that was entered, along with a painting of Camille. It is believed that the exhibition was a success. Around that time, he became even more interested in mixing elements of industrialization and the man-made environment with natural and undeveloped surroundings. By combining rustic charm with technology, such as factory chimneys, trains or bridges, he was revolutionizing the art of landscape painting.

INCREASING INTEREST

In 1873, Monet's profits doubled compared with previous years. His work at the time reflects his renewed energy and optimism and Durand-Ruel

LE JAPONISME

Monet claimed that he bought the first Japanese prints that were shipped to Le Havre in 1856. Since then he had collected further wood-block prints and the flat, asymmetrical and brightly coloured compositions continued to influence his art. From the 1850s changes had occurred in Japan's political and social structure and it opened its borders to international trade. In 1867, the Exposition Universelle in Paris introduced even more people to the arts of Japan and the impact was huge for many avant-garde European artists and designers. Paris became the primary European location for Japanese art and artefacts and several Japanese art dealers moved in. The expression 'Le Japonisme' was first used by Jules Claretie in his book *L'Art Français en 1872*.

and Latouche responded accordingly. His proximity to Paris meant that he could still meet with his fellow artists at the Café Guerbois and keep up with latest thoughts and ideas, while Renoir often joined him at Argenteuil and the two painters would go on painting expeditions around the countryside. Whatever his theme at this time, Monet began focusing on painting dull and bright lights at differing times of day or night and across the seasons. Manet was also a visitor to Argenteuil.

In 1872 and 1873, Monet returned to Normandy, where he painted many landscapes and seascapes of Étretat, Le Havre and Saint-Adresse.

Above right: Claude Monet Reading, *Renoir, 1872. This picture is indicative of a close friendship; Monet was clearly at ease while Renoir worked.*

Right: Portrait of Madame Claude Monet, *Renoir, 1872. Renoir painted this portrait at the same time as he painted Monet reading his newspaper. Monet kept both portraits for the rest of his life, as reminders of happy times.*

THE FIRST EXHIBITION

In 1874, Monet and his friends held what they called The First Exhibition of the Société Anonyme des Artistes. Not a successful exhibition, it nevertheless changed the lives of several of the exhibitors and the course of art history.

Monet's output during 1872 and 1873 was extremely varied. He painted fruit trees, frosts and snow effects, figures, flowers and of course, rivers and the sea.

STUDIO IN PARIS
Toward the end of 1873, a photographer, Gaspard-Félix Tournachon (1820–1910), who was known as Nadar, invited Monet to work from his studio, which was on the second floor of 35 boulevard des Capucines in Paris.

Below: The Museum at Le Havre, 1873. *This view is taken from the harbour looking across to the Musée des Beaux-Arts.*

Much earlier, the idea of having an independent exhibition away from the official Salon had been discussed by Bazille, Monet and several of the friends who went painting in the forest of Fontainebleau. The idea was discarded when they realized how expensive and difficult it would be, but by 1873, it had surfaced again. Monet, Renoir, Boudin, Sisley, Pissarro, Cézanne, Degas, Berthe Morisot (1841–95) and some other artists, most of whom were disillusioned with the Salon and weary of battling to have their work accepted for it, banded together, called themselves the 'Société Anonyme des

Artistes' and arranged their own exhibition. They did not intend to promote any particular style of art, but simply to invite people to see and appreciate their work.

CRITICS' RESPONSES
The exhibition, although held at a time when Parisians wanted to be uplifted, was not successful. There were 175 visitors on the first day and over the month the total attendance was around 3,500. Despite this, it received wide press coverage. Some critics were positive, but the most memorable reviews were contemptuous, attacking

THE FIRST IMPRESSIONIST EXHIBITION

The First Exhibition of the Société Anonyme des Artistes was opened at the photographer Nadar's former studio on 15 April 1874 and lasted one month. (There were to be eight exhibitions from 1874–86.) Admission was 1 franc and the catalogue cost 50 centimes. All members of the Société Anonyme paid 60 francs a year to belong and for this, all had equal rights. Renoir chaired the committee that arranged the hanging. There were 165 works in the exhibition, including five oil paintings and seven pastels by Monet. Monet's paintings included *Le Havre: Fishing Boats Leaving the Harbour, Boulevard des Capucines, Poppies* and *Impression, Sunrise.*

Right: Boulevard des Capucines, *1873–74. Movement is captured in the flicking brushstrokes, to create blurred figures.*

the unfinished quality of the paintings. Taking the name derisively from Monet's painting of *Le Havre* of 1872, the artist and critic Louis Leroy wrote scornfully in the magazine *Le Charivari*, about "The Exhibition of the Impressionists", proclaiming that Monet's painting could hardly be called a finished work. Another writer, Émile Cardon in *La Presse* wrote derisively about the "School of Impressionism" and an unsigned review in *La Patrie* read "Looking at the first rough works – and rough is the right word – you simply shrug your shoulders; seeing the next lot, you burst out laughing; but with the last ones you finally get angry. And you are sorry you did not give the franc you paid to get in to some poor beggar." If nothing else, the exhibition had at least gained some publicity.

Right: Claude Monet Painting in His Garden at Argenteuil, *Renoir, 1873. In this picture, Renoir created an intimate image of his friend.*

THE FLOATING STUDIO

Undeterred by the negative reactions of critics, Monet spent the summer of 1874 painting with more determination and livelier colours. Always happy near water, he especially enjoyed painting his canvases from a floating studio boat.

After several turbulent years, Monet seemed to have become reconciled to the hostility his work generated in some quarters and refused to let this discourage him. He had not sold any work at the independent exhibition that spring, but was still selling some work through Durand-Ruel and a few other dealers and buyers.

TRANQUILLITY
Since the Franco-Prussian War, Monet's income had increased and he was contented at Argenteuil with Camille and Jean and spent much of the time with them. He also took pleasure in the company of other painters, particularly working with Renoir.

At times that summer, they were also joined by Manet, who, since his early antagonism, had become Monet's friend. He retained his reservations toward the group, but discovered that he enjoyed painting *en plein air* with them. Manet's work from that year was the closest he came to their style, with summery scenes around the Seine executed in bright colours. Renoir too, seems to have been inspired to integrate some of Monet's innovative ideas in his own work. That year, Monet painted nearly 40 canvases.

CONTRASTING COMPOSITIONS
In addition to skies, water and foliage, Monet continued producing compositions that included bridges, boats, buildings and promenades. More than ever, he seemed to take pleasure in incorporating modern technological achievements and architecture within natural surroundings. Again, this inspired his friends and colleagues who began assimilating contemporary buildings within their landscapes. Monet's critics frequently called attention to the incomplete and unfinished quality of his paintings. But this was intentional;

he set out to purposefully create the appearance of spontaneity and immediacy. One of his skills was in creating compositions that draw viewers in and around his pictures. Contrasting horizontals with verticals and diagonals, interspersing curves with straight lines, applying short and longer marks and light and dark colours were all part of his decisions over where certain elements would achieve maximum interest. The ways in which he cropped, repeated and overlapped certain

Above: Camille and Jean Monet in the Garden at Argenteuil, *1873. Focusing on the dappling light, Monet captured an unusual family moment.*

components in his work also demonstrates the continuing influence of Japanese woodcut prints.

A UNIQUE VIEW
The river was always a lure to Monet and many of his works from that time were painted from his boat, which he had recently bought and converted into

a floating studio. Based on one that had been used by Daubigny, Monet kept his moored near his home and he often rowed it along the Seine to obtain a unique view from the water. He would take Camille with him, and sometimes painted the boat itself from the bank to study shadow and reflection. Manet, who painted Monet on his floating studio, grandly described him as "the Raphael of water".

Below: Boats, Regatta at Argenteuil, *c.1874. In this painting, fragmented brushstrokes catch the vibrant play of light and reflections on the water.*

Bottom: The Monet Family in their Garden at Argenteuil, *Manet, 1874, painted while Manet was staying with the Monets.*

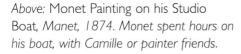

Above: Monet Painting on his Studio Boat, *Manet, 1874. Monet spent hours on his boat, with Camille or painter friends.*

FLUCTUATING INCOME

As his earnings increased, Monet hired a maid and a gardener, ordered good wines and moved into a larger house in Argenteuil. Then in 1875, financial pressures ensuing from the First Impressionist Exhibition meant that he, Renoir, Sisley and Morisot had to auction several paintings. Journalist friends announced the auction and made constructive observations about it, but they were unable to influence buyers and sales were poor. The public complained that the works were overpriced, or they found them amusing, and although Monet auctioned 20 paintings, he only managed to sell a few works at extremely reduced prices. His income for 1875 was down on previous years and he appealed to Manet for help. Through Manet's influence, several friends and acquaintances bought paintings from him, including Manet himself. Impressionism, however, was not catching on with the public.

THE SECOND EXHIBITION

In terms of Monet's career, two particularly significant events occurred in 1876. The first was a meeting with Victor Chocquet (1821–96), in which he offered his apartment as a studio; the second was the next Impressionist exhibition that took place in April.

In February 1876, Cézanne introduced his patron Chocquet to Monet. Chocquet was an official in the Customs Service. He was not rich, but he greatly admired Renoir's and Cézanne's paintings and bought them even while others ridiculed them. At their introduction, he immediately bought one of Monet's sketches and a pastel. He became a firm supporter and at the Second Impressionist Exhibition that year, he pointed out the positive aspects of the paintings to unenthused visitors. He also invited Monet to paint from his apartment in Paris.

THE NEXT EXHIBITION

In the year that Alexander Graham Bell invented the telephone, the second independent exhibition opened on 11 April at Durand-Ruel's gallery in the rue le Peletier in Paris. As Impressionism was still a term of abuse, the artists ignored the title and called

Above: Tow-Path at Argenteuil, c.1875. Using short, choppy brushstrokes, Monet conveyed a winter's day with a hint of spring.

the exhibition *La Deuxième Exposition de Peinture*. Some of the more conventional artists who had taken part in the first show abstained from the second, so the number of exhibitors dropped from 30 to 20.

As it was, some of those who did exhibit had no connection with Impressionism, but one newcomer who did, caused a sensation. He was Gustave Caillebotte (1848–94), a wealthy young man who had met Monet and Renoir in Argenteuil and had been introduced to the rest of the group by them. He had been involved in the organization of the 1874 exhibition, but by 1876, he decided to take part. His paintings, and in particular *The Floor Strippers*, were remarked upon and admired greatly by visitors and critics. Consequently he took part in the later exhibitions of the Impressionist group as well.

Below: Double page from Monet's account book detailing the sales of his paintings, December 1874–March 1875.

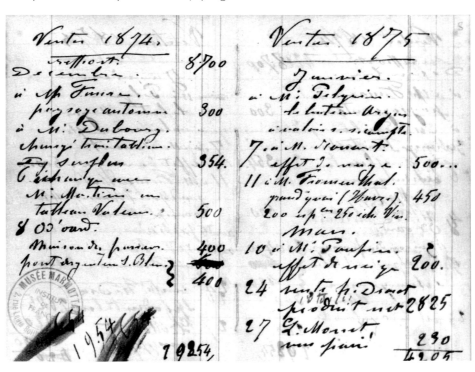

PAINTING PARKS

Monet had spent time painting the colour and atmosphere of the countryside and gardens of Argenteuil, but for some time he had not executed many works in Paris. During the spring of 1876, he worked in the rue de Rivoli and produced four paintings of the Tuileries Gardens. At about the same time, he also painted five views of the Parc Monceau. His paintings of parks of that period show his varied working methods; some are lightly worked, while others are more finished.

Monet submitted 18 works to the exhibition, among those was a large, uncharacteristic canvas, titled *The Japanese Girl* in which Camille posed wearing a kimono and a blonde wig and holding a fan. It reflects his admiration of Japanese culture and art, although he later dismissed it as "a heap of rubbish". Nevertheless, the painting was one of the commercial successes of the exhibition and sold for 2,000 francs. Monet also included paintings of figures in the open air, such as *Woman with a Parasol, Madame Monet and Her Son* that he painted the previous year. The painting was more about the effects of the breeze than the figures. The second exhibition attracted greater journalistic

Above: The Floor Strippers, *Caillebotte, 1875. This was the sensation of the Second Impressionist Exhibition in 1876, although it was not included in the catalogue. Admirers marvelled at the realism of three men renovating a floor.*

Above: La Japonaise, *1876. Monet used brilliant colour and Japanese elements for this painting he produced of Camille Monet dressed in a Japanese costume.*

exposure than the first and although some lacked respect, there were more positive comments too. It appears that opinions about the finish of paintings remained largely as they had before the Franco-Prussian War, but some reviewers were changing and more approving observations on the originality and brilliance of his landscape paintings were noted. Through the modest profits earned from visitors and

the sale of work, the group was able to pay Durand-Ruel 3,000 francs for the use of his gallery for the month. Despite the relative success of the exhibition, Monet was still concerned about his financial stability.

THE GARE SAINT-LAZARE

Over the course of 1876, Monet again experienced financial difficulties. The proceeds from his paintings had dropped and he could not meet the increasing demands of his lifestyle and family. However, the following year, his paintings of railway scenes were well received.

Monet often took the train for Argenteuil or Normandy from the Gare Saint-Lazare. Fascinated by the bustle of the place, he began making negotiations to paint this image of modernity. In January of 1877, he took up residence in a studio rented by Caillebotte in rue Moncey, leaving Camille in Argenteuil as Jean was now attending school.

THE STATION

Calling it a campaign, Monet worked from both the studio and on site, painting a series of views of the outside and inside of the Gare Saint-Lazare. Trains and railways had been depicted in earlier Impressionist works (and by Turner in *Rain, Steam and Speed*, c.1844), but were not generally regarded as suitable subjects for fine art. These works were precursors to Monet's later serial paintings, showing the same subjects in changing lights at different times of day.

From this station, trains headed for Rouen, Argenteuil, Bougival, Pontoise, Vétheuil and other favourite spots of the Impressionist painters. The station and trains were symbols of industrial progress and, in painting them, Monet showed the establishment that he was a man of his time.

The busy station was a modern structure of iron, steel and glass that along with other similar stations, had been nicknamed 'the new cathedrals of France'. Obtaining permission to paint right inside the building, he produced several preliminary sketches, planning the compositions of straight and diagonal lines contrasting with soft, rounded forms and shapes. He also positioned himself farther away, opposite the metal structure of the Pont de l'Europe and depicted the engines with their plumes of smoke.

THE THIRD IMPRESSIONIST EXHIBITION

The third exhibition in 1877 brought no improvement to the artists' financial position, but it was the most important as they had decided to establish themselves as one coherent and clearly

THE EFFECTS OF STEAM AND LIGHT

Monet did not focus on individual elements, such as people or trains, but he emphasized the effects of steam and light. The paintings resemble interior landscapes, with smoke from the engines creating the same effect as clouds in the sky. Swift brushstrokes record each element, from the engines to the crowd of passengers on the platform. The high glass-canopied ceiling and network of windows and rails contrast with the billowing clouds of smoke and rising steam of the locomotives. Monet completed 11 paintings of this subject in all. Ernest Hoschedé bought some of the works, others were purchased by individual buyers and Monet kept four. He exhibited seven of the railway station canvases in the Third Impressionist Exhibition, which opened in April, 1877.

recognizable group and so at last adopted the term Impressionism. Eighteen artists took part in the show, which was organized and financed by Caillebotte. Held in a five-room apartment opposite Durand-Ruel's gallery in the rue le Peletier, it lasted from 4–30 April 1877. Monet, still in dire straits financially, exhibited 30 paintings. They were received fairly well, particularly his Gare Saint-Lazare paintings, which were described as a true wonder in the magazine *L'Homme Libre*. "Monet's paintbrush has represented not only the movement, the colour and the activity, but also the

Left: The Gare St. Lazare, 1877. Monet persuaded the officials to have the Rouen train delayed so the light would be better.

Above: The Arrival of the Normandy Train, Gare Saint-Lazare, 1877. *This painting was described as "magnificent".*

Below: Exterior of the Gare Saint-Lazare, Arrival of a Train, 1877. *Monet's stations were full of steam and light.*

rejoicing. It is unforgettable. The station, of course, is full of noise-screeches, whistles – audible through the confusion of the clouds of grey and blue smoke. It is a pictorial symphony." Zola also praised the paintings: "Monsieur Claude Monet is the strongest personality in the group. This year he has exhibited some superb railway station scenes. You can hear the rumbling of the trains pulling in and see the smoke rolling under the vast sheds. That is painting today, in these beautifully broad, modern frames. Our artists must find the poetry in railway stations, just as their fathers found it in forests and rivers."

A short-lived journal called *L'Impressioniste* was published to coincide with the third exhibition. Its purpose was to try to defend Impressionists from the critical attack they had come to expect during the run of the exhibition.

ARGENTEUIL AND PARIS

The Third Impressionist Exhibition had provoked mixed reviews; there were the usual criticisms, but support came from some critics, including the writer Zola. Ernest Hoschedé, Monet's patron at Montgeron, went bankrupt, selling Monet's canvases to pay off debts.

vision, no choice of motifs which show you something of the man and something of the artist. One seeks in vain for a thought and for a soul behind this eye and this hand." Another reporter, Albert Wolff, who wrote for *Le Figaro*, said: "Rue le Peletier is having a run of bad luck. First there was the fire at the opera house and now Fate has struck again. An exhibition of so-called art has just opened at Durand-Ruel's. Five or six lunatics, blinded by ambition…have put their work on show. These self-appointed artists call themselves rebels, Impressionists: they take a canvas, brush and paint, fling on the colours indiscriminately and then sign the thing." Nevertheless, respected writers and critics were also beginning

Left: A Corner of the Garden at Montgeron, 1876–77, one of the paintings of the Hoschedés' garden.

With the Third Impressionist Exhibition, for the first time, the group began to achieve greater approval from some quarters. Most of the artists had not been in favour of exhibiting as a single entity, feeling that they were unique and distinctive, but they realized that unless they pulled together, they would risk being targeted individually by hostile critics. As a unified group, they stood stronger against detractors.

CONFLICTING OPINIONS

One of the main criticisms of the Impressionists' work was that it was a mechanical reproduction of direct observations. In 1877 one reviewer wrote "There is no intimate sentiment, no delicacy of impression, no personal

Right: Gladioli, c.1876. With a jewel-bright palette, Monet captured a corner of the garden at Argenteuil.

to champion them. Zola, for instance, again indulging in art criticism, wrote: "I think one has to understand Impressionist painters as painters who paint reality and who presume to render the very impression of nature, who do not concentrate on details but on the whole. It is true that at 20 paces from the painting one cannot clearly distinguish the nose or the eyes of a character; to render him as one sees it, one must not paint him with his wrinkles, but in the life of his attitude, with the vibrating air that surrounds him." This kind of support and recognition must have heartened the artists who by then had been striving to achieve something worthwhile for many years.

CAMILLE'S ILLNESS

Early in 1877, when Monet was spending so much time in Paris, Camille had started to become ill. The local doctor at Argenteuil had called in another for a second opinion and an operation was discussed, but in the end it did not take place. An admirer and patron of Monet's work, Dr Georges de Bellio, is thought to have given his advice on this. Camille was also pregnant with their second child and it is believed that the symptoms of her illness only became apparent after this, or the couple would not have risked the pregnancy knowing that she was ill.

ERNEST HOSCHEDÉ

The Parisian department store owner, Ernest Hoschedé (1837–91), had been buying Monet's work since 1874. In 1876, he had commissioned Monet to paint large decorative panels for his home, the Château de Rottembourg in Montgeron and other smaller works. Hoschedé continued as a patron until August 1877, when he went bankrupt and the following June, his art collection was auctioned off. Included in this were 16 canvases by Monet, which were sold at very low prices. Hoschedé's collapse accelerated Monet's monetary problems and his debts accumulated. He wrote to Manet and Zola asking for help to avoid his family's eviction from the house in Argenteuil.

Top: The Turkeys at the Château de Rottembourg, Montgeron, *1877, was one of many that Monet painted for Hoschedé.*

Above: Painted while in Paris, View over the Tuileries Gardens, *1876, shows the subtle changes of light and perspective.*

LEAVING ARGENTEUIL

In January 1878, Monet and his family left Argenteuil and moved to Paris for a short time. For the third Paris Exposition Universelle, Monet painted two bright, cheerful pictures of the crowds lining the streets. With the Hoschedés, Monet and his family moved to Vétheuil.

Very slowly, Monet and other Impressionists were achieving some recognition for their efforts.

THE IMPRESSIONIST PAINTERS

In May 1878, the critic Théodore Duret wrote a booklet called *The Impressionist Painters*. He asserted that the Impressionists were attracting constructive reviews by several important critics and writers and that the public's opinion of them was becoming favourable. Naming Corot, Courbet and Manet as their precursors, he described the Impressionists' development through *plein air* painting and applying some of the techniques of Japanese art. Praising Monet as the "Impressionist par excellence", he wrote: "Claude Monet has succeeded in fixing the fugitive images that his predecessors had neglected or considered impossible to render with the brush. The thousand nuances which inflect the water of the sea or rivers, the play of light in clouds, the vibrant colours of flowers and the spangled reflections of leaves in the rays of a fiery sun, have been seized by him in all their truth." Although it did not have a huge impact, this booklet was nevertheless a particularly positive piece of publicity.

VÉTHEUIL

In March, Monet wrote to Hoschedé: "My wife has just had another baby and I find myself penniless and unable to pay for the medical care that both mother

EXPOSITION UNIVERSELLE

The third Exposition Universelle was held in Paris in 1878, from May to November. Intended to celebrate the recovery of France after its defeat in the Franco-Prussian War, it was the largest world fair ever held. After initial problems with the preparations, the French exhibits filled half, with other countries' exhibits filling the remaining area. To make sure that everyone joined in the festivities, a national holiday was declared on 30 June and Monet captured the crowds and holiday mood of Paris with two lively paintings of the colourful, festooned streets in rue Montorgueil and rue Saint-Denis. As with the Gare Saint-Lazare paintings, the emphasis is on the movement and atmosphere, rather than on the people in the picture. Oddly, the recently bankrupted Hoschedé bought one of the paintings that July.

Right: The Rue Montorgueil, Celebration of June 30, 1878, one of two streets painted to celebrate the Exhibition. Monet created effects of sunlight, shade and movement.

home, took care of all their children and helped to look after Camille. Alice also contributed money from her own funds to pay off some of Monet's pressing debts. Hoschedé found it hard to accept his newly impoverished circumstances, however, and refused to dismiss his servants even though he could no longer pay them. He also retained his Parisian apartment, although his mother paid for that. Throughout this period, Monet worked ceaselessly, painting many views of Vétheuil in inclement weather conditions, even though the winter was exceptionally severe.

and child must have." Camille, by then suffering from a chronic illness, was desperately ill, and had given birth to a second son, Michel, in March 1878, which weakened her even more. Their first son, Jean, was a little more than 10 years old at the time.

In September of that year, Monet rented a house for his family on the southern edge of Vétheuil, a quiet village on the banks of the River Seine nearly 40 miles (64km) north of Paris.

SHARED HOUSEHOLD

Shortly after settling there, Hoschedé turned to Monet for help and the two men agreed that he, his wife Alice and their six children, should share the house at Vétheuil with the Monet family to share costs and to help alleviate some of their financial problems. It was also a positive move for Monet as Alice ran the

Top left: Colour print of a view of the Exposition Universelle of 1878 in Paris. The largest exhibition of its type, it covered more than 0.27 sq km (66 acres).

Above: Entrance to the Village of Vétheuil in Winter, 1880. Monet has captured a chilly, snowy scene, which reflected the unhappiness he was feeling about his wife and his poverty.

Left: Frost near Vétheuil, 1880. At this sad time in his life, Monet captures the bleakness of the world with this luminous picture of frosty weather.

A DIFFICULT TIME

Monet's output during the winter of 1878 to 1879 and the following spring was almost frenzied. Nearing 40, he realized that his status in the established art world had not advanced in the way he would have hoped.

Although many of Monet's letters from this period frequently lament his problems, his production continued unabated. From his studio boat, he painted views around Vétheuil, a town that had not yet succumbed to industrialization and so he once again focused on natural forms and phenomena.

DESPERATE STRAITS

Monet was despairing about his financial state. On 30 December 1878, he wrote to de Bellio, "I am not a beginner anymore and it is dreadful to be in such a position at my age, forever begging and pestering buyers. As the year ends I am doubly aware of my misfortune, for '79 is beginning as this year has ended, in utter despondency, especially with regard to my dear ones, to whom I have not been able to give even the smallest present."

Above: Vétheuil, *1879. This is an unusually shimmering painting that Monet painted at this time of great sorrow.*

FREEZING LANDSCAPES

That winter, he once more braved the elements, producing several paintings that show the intense cold and dullness of the light. His paintings of that time contain neither living creature nor golden sunlit skies. Instead, the desolate landscapes around him feature cold, grey, icy tones. As ever he was painting what he saw in front of him, including the freezing over of the Seine, but also at this time, his own despair and anguish seems to have emerged in his paintings.

He tried to maintain a positive outlook, but it was difficult. In May 1879, he wrote to Hoschedé in Paris: "I am totally discouraged...I must accept the hard fact that I cannot hope to earn enough money from my paintings to pay for our life here at Vétheuil....We can't be very good company for you and Madame

Left: The Church at Vétheuil under Snow, *1878–79. Unlike some other snow scenes, this does not include warm tints.*

Right: Camille on her Deathbed, 1879. *Monet painted quickly and automatically, capturing the image of his beloved wife.*

Hoschedé, myself more and more embittered and my wife, nearly always sick."

CAMILLE

Having endured her husband's erratic income and condemnation by his family, Camille Monet showed no signs of recovery. Her health had been worsening since the birth of Michel in March 1878 and by the late summer of the following year, it was clear that she would not recover. She had been Monet's faithful companion for 13 years and had been his only model, whether in green taffeta, white voile or a red kimono, with him on his studio boat, in fields and gardens or on beaches. On 5 September 1879, she died, aged 32, leaving a grieving husband and two small sons. As he sat by her deathbed, Monet felt compelled to reach for his paints and sketch her. He later confided in a friend: "I found myself at daybreak at the bedside of a woman who had been and always will be dear to me. My gaze was fixed on her tragic temples and I caught myself observing the shades and nuances of colour Death brought to her countenance. Blues, yellows, greys, I don't know what. That is the state I was in. The wish came upon me, quite naturally, to record the image of her who was departing from us forever. But before it occurred to me to draw those features I knew and loved so well, I felt an automatic, organic response to the shock of the colours….Pity me, my friend." On the same day, he wrote to de Bellio: "My poor wife died this morning …I am filled with dismay to find myself alone with my poor children." He put money in the letter and asked de Bellio to redeem a medallion of Camille's that he had pawned as he wanted to put it around her neck "before she leaves us". Weeks later, he wrote to other friends, describing his continuing grief.

Right: The Church at Vétheuil, 1879. *This wintry scene of the church has a warmer feeling owing to some red tints.*

A MATURING STYLE

From the moment of Camille's death, Monet seemed to leave his earlier style behind and focus more on the unspoiled, raw aspects of nature. No weather effects seemed to be too severe or wild; no situation was too difficult or daunting. In other words, rather than sinking under the weight of his worries and woes, he eventually emerged as a mature, stronger and more accomplished artist. He began travelling across France more, so that he could extend the range of his painting. In later life, he described his desire to travel and paint: "I felt the need in order to widen my field of observation and to refresh my vision."

Above: View of Bordighera, Italy, 1884. *Monet produced some of his best, most mature work in the early 1880s with his landscapes and seascapes.* Left: The Walk, 1882, *is a sketch depicting the Hoschedé girls walking along a coastal cliff path in summer. In this picture, Monet uses a palette of soft tones of blue, pink and lilac in contrast to the chilly tones in earlier paintings.*

DESPAIR AND HOPE

In the April before Camille died, Monet had reluctantly joined in with the Fourth Impressionist Exhibition. Once again, Caillebotte organized it all, but Monet's melancholy prevented him from entering wholeheartedly into the spirit of the event.

Albert Wolff, a journalist at *Le Figaro*, commented on Monet's work at the Fourth Impressionist exhibition: "M. Monet has sent 29 landscapes that look as if they were done in a single afternoon....He is stuck in this mess and will never get out."

PAINTING INSIDE

Still grief-stricken following Camille's death, Monet often worked indoors – a departure from his work in recent years. He completed unfinished pictures and added to some that had been the subject of particularly scathing reviews. More than at any other time in his career, he also produced several still life paintings, mainly arrangements of fruit and flowers in quite thick, controlled brushstrokes and colourful paint. After his melancholic frozen scenes of winter in Vétheuil, these brightly coloured paintings possibly indicate that he had decided to make an effort to face the future with some of his old determination.

Above: Still Life with Pears and Grapes, *1880. With complementary colour juxtapositions, Monet made these luscious fruits even more vibrant.*

Above: Sunflowers, *1881. The contrast of the golden flowers against the blue-violet background creates an intensity that influenced the post-Impressionist painter Vincent van Gogh.*

THE FROZEN SEINE

The winter of 1879 to 1880 was even colder than the preceding one, with temperatures dropping to -25°C (-77°F). The Seine froze over again, this time so thickly that it could be crossed on foot. Monet set up his easel outside and painted the icy scenes before him, applying short, stubby brushmarks in mellow and subdued colours. The frost and ice did not last as long as the previous year, and by January, he captured the spectacular thaw, showing the slow movements of the ice floes on the still river and the cold, clear air.

EXHIBITING AGAIN

Throughout that year, creditors for both Hoschedé and Monet frequently called at the house. Monet decided that he had to try a different approach. Going against the rest of the Impressionist group, he declined to participate in the Fifth Impressionist Exhibition. This caused bad feeling among several of his friends and colleagues, but he had determined to try and be accepted in more conventional circles since the independent route was not working.

After 10 years of avoiding it, he resolved to submit some work to the Salon jury once more. He presented two paintings there in 1880, *Sunset on the Seine at Lavacourt* and *Break Up of the Ice near Vétheuil*. The Lavacourt painting was accepted, but the Vétheuil canvas was rejected. Hierarchy of display meant that *Sunset on the Seine at Lavacourt* was displayed on the least esteemed upper row and brought him little positive feedback. However, the publisher of the magazine *La Vie Moderne* invited him to exhibit his work in the journal's offices, and this was his first one-man show.

THE FOURTH IMPRESSIONIST EXHIBITION

With 15 participants, the exhibition opened on 10 April 1879 at 28 avenue l'Opéra. Monet had submitted 29 works, which were displayed with 38 works by Pissarro in the last room. As Camille was extremely ill at the time, Monet did not attend the exhibition and Cézanne, Renoir and Sisley did not participate at all. Attendance was better than at the Third Impressionist Exhibition, but sales were low. Admission was 50 centimes and by the end of the exhibition on 11 May, all expenses had been covered and participants received about 440 francs. Once more, the critics were hostile, although the public was less critical. Most reviewers complained that the Impressionists were no longer a cohesive group, which was justified as most of the artists wanted to be seen as independent and unique.

Before the exhibition, Monet was interviewed by one of the magazine's contributors, Emile Taboureux. He tried to describe his methods to Taboureux: "I don't understand how people can shut themselves in a room. To draw, yes; to paint, no." He then gesticulated to the entire landscape of Vétheuil, exclaiming: "There is my studio!"

Above: Sunset on the Seine at Lavacourt, Winter Effect *1880. This river scene was accepted by the Salon jury and exhibited at the Salon of 1880.*

Below: Banks of the Seine, Vétheuil, *1880. This picture was part of a series showing the river at different times of day, in varying weather conditions. It was probably finished in the studio.*

ON THE MOVE AGAIN

Despite the relative success of his one-man exhibition at the offices of *La Vie Moderne*, Monet's financial situation was barely improved since many of the works shown had already been bought from him and were simply lent for the show.

Monet was still despondent, but with the encouragement of his friends and extended family, he continued to paint.

HIGHS AND LOWS

Monet spent the rest of 1880 working in and around Vétheuil, still finding plenty of subjects to paint. He occasionally repeated views that he had painted in previous years, but always in different light effects and he found new views of old locations, such as Lavacourt seen through the willow leaves.

In August 1880, one of his Lecadre cousins invited him to take part in an exhibition in Le Havre. Pleased to return to his roots, he submitted

Above: Fruit Tarts, 1882. *With his usual care and attention to detail when painting still lifes, this image of fruit tarts, freshly made and ready to be eaten, glistens with colour and texture.*

several paintings, but was rewarded with derisory reviews in the local press. This seems a particularly hostile reaction. The inhabitants of Le Havre clearly did not care that he had been a local boy.

Right: Garden at Vétheuil, 1881. *Monet had loved gardens since he was a young boy. He cultivated this at Vétheuil and made much of the dappled sunlight on the path.*

Above: This black and white photograph c.1880, shows both the Monet and Hoschedé families relaxing in the garden.

Above: Boat Lying at Low Tide, 1881. Retaining his understanding of composition and contrast, Monet seems just as occupied with creating a surface texture as he is by building up light and shade.

The following month he spent time with his brother Léon who was a great admirer of his work, firstly in Rouen, and then at Léon's cottage in the resort of Petites-Dalles near Fécamp in Normandy. Noted for its dramatically high cliffs and shingled stretches of beach, the work Monet produced there was sketchy and expressive.

Over the next two years he attracted several new admirers and patrons. One, Frederick Delius, paid 1,400 francs for two still lifes of fruits. The dealer Georges Petit (1856–1920) who was a rival of Durand-Ruel, had been buying work directly from him and from Hoschedé since 1878, but that year, he hardly bought any works. Sales of Monet's paintings continued to fluctuate broadly. For instance, in September 1880, he sold a painting for 250 francs and in October, he sold another for 2,380 francs. Overall though, his income for 1880 was higher than in the previous two years. By 1881, Durand-Ruel's business had recovered sufficiently from the financial problems he had been experiencing and he resumed his buying of Monet's work and advancing him expenses. Monet was beginning to have more success selling his paintings.

LIFE AT HOME

Monet had grown close to Alice Hoschedé while she brought up her six and his two children at Vétheuil and her husband remained in Paris. She worked hard to keep the household running, at times on practically no money at all. Villagers gossiped about the uncommon arrangement, but Monet seems to have brushed off any disapproving looks or comments. He spent more time at home when the weather was particularly bad, painting the garden, portraits of the children or still lifes of flowers and fruit. Incessant rain during the autumn and further cold winter weather prompted a series of paintings of the resulting floods when the ice thawed and the Seine burst its banks.

MOVE TO POISSY

By the time Monet returned to Vétheuil from Fécamp, the decision to move again had almost been made for him. He and Alice had not been able to pay the rent for some time and the local people were growing antagonistic toward them because of their unusual domestic arrangements. It was not conventional for a widower to live with another man's wife and for the two families to share children, however contented they all might have seemed with the situation. Ernest Hoschedé the estranged husband, was living a bachelor's life in Paris and does not

MARINE PAINTINGS

Monet's marine paintings had achieved particular success during the previous year, so he decided to return to Fécamp and paint more of them. In all these works, he continued applying the especially loose and animated brushstrokes that he had used previously, despite the fact that this method had always been the most criticized aspect of his work.

seem to have been interested in his wife and children. In December, 1881, Monet, Alice and all the children moved to Poissy, a small industrial town on the Seine to the west of Argenteuil, about 20km (12.5 miles) from Paris. This triggered even more speculation about their relationship. While Alice had remained in the house at Vétheuil after Camille's death, helping Monet come to terms with his grief and taking care of his children, it was acceptable. By following him to Poissy, it shed a different light on their liaison and it became a full-blown scandal.

TRAVELLING TO THE COAST

Although the house in Poissy was comfortable and had a fine view of the Seine, Monet felt uninspired. The town held no appeal for him and so after only two months, as early as February 1882, he left to set off for Dieppe on the Normandy coast.

Monet was able to satisfy his passion for nature painting the seascapes of Pourville, Étretat and Varengeville. In these works he continues his idea of painting the same motif under changing light and weather conditions.

PAINTING THE COAST

Monet travelled around Normandy in search of appealing views, determined to make enough money to support Jean and Michel as well as Alice and the six Hoschedé children. He began by painting in Dieppe, but soon moved on to Pourville, a small fishing village not far away and Varengeville – another area full of spectacular cliffs, shingled beaches and choppy seas. He frequently created simplified compositions, and tried to represent the textures and shapes of the elements as patterns on his canvases. His preference for painting landscapes and seascapes with the absence of the human element was clear as his concerns for the perception of light effects took precedence. Wrapped up against the biting winds

and clutching his paintbrush on cliffs and promontories, he began focusing less on the river and more on the sea.

THE SEVENTH IMPRESSIONIST EXHIBITION

As Monet was busily painting around the Normandy coast, the other artists of the Impressionist group were

Above: Pourville, Villa Juliette, 1882. Monet rented the villa for his extended family from June to October in 1882.

discussing their next joint exhibition. He had missed the last two, but on his return to Poissy, Pissarro persuaded him to take part in the next one. There were many disagreements, with some artists insisting that they either would or would not take part if other individuals did or did not participate. For instance, Monet would only contribute if Renoir and Caillebotte did also and Morisot maintained that she would only submit work if Monet agreed to join them. Durand-Ruel stepped in as arbitrator and on 1 March 1882, the Seventh Impressionist Exhibition, this time called the *Septième Exposition des Artistes Indépendants*, opened at the Salons du Panorama de Reichshoffen at 251 rue St-Honoré in Paris. The building had come to be accepted as a suitable space for art exhibitions, even though part of it was taken up with a

Left: The Beach at Pourville, Setting Sun, 1882. This picture shows Monet's restraint and removal of the superfluous.

panorama that depressingly depicted one of the greatest defeats suffered by the French during the Franco-Prussian War. Only nine artists took part and Durand-Ruel filled the rooms with many of the works he had bought from them previously, offering them at high prices to create an image of prestige. Monet was represented by 35 paintings, mainly of seascapes, landscapes and still lifes.

This time, most reviews of the exhibition were positive, if cautious. Criticism ranged from the artists' styles being indistinguishable from each other, to their colours being too wild and unnatural. Praise included the writings of Ernest Chesneau in *Paris-Journal*, specifically describing Monet's marine paintings: "I stop before these admirable seascapes in which, for the first time, I see rendered with such extraordinary power of illusion – the upswells and long descending sighs of the ocean, the rivulets of the eddying waves, the glaucous surface of the deep water and the violet hues of the low tide above its bed of sand."

HOLIDAY

The situation between Hoschedé, Monet and Alice had become difficult. Alice still insisted that Hoschedé paid for her and his children, even though Monet was also trying to support them. Financially,

Below: The Gorge at Varengeville, *1882. In February 1882, Monet discovered the charms of Pourville and Varengeville.*

Above: Vase of Flowers, *c.1881–82. Using small brushes and building up the paint, Monet retained the softness of the petals.*

Alice was struggling and several of the children had fallen ill. As an antidote to their problems, from June to October, Monet rented a villa in Pourville for him, Alice and the children. With renewed vigour, he painted several colourful and sweeping pictures of the area and he gave Blanche Hoschedé (1865–1947) the Hoschedés' second daughter, her first painting lessons.

As had become characteristic, he veered from exhilaration to misery throughout the holiday. When he was with the family or painting feverishly, he was extremely happy, but when he remembered the debts that he would be facing back at Poissy, or if the weather was too harsh to paint in (as it frequently was that summer) despair overwhelmed him.

MOVING TO GIVERNY

In January 1883, Durand-Ruel proposed a scheme whereby he would organize a solo exhibition for each of the Impressionists. In the same month, Monet went to stay first in Le Havre and then in Étretat to produce some canvases for the exhibition.

Durand-Ruel's proposal was as exciting as it was helpful. This independent show would help to raise Monet's profile and get him noticed by dealers.

THE ONE-MAN EXHIBITION

Delighted with the striking views at Étretat, Monet produced several more of his seascapes that were proving so popular. On 1 March, his solo show opened at Durand-Ruel's gallery in the boulevard de la Madeleine in Paris. He was the first of the group to have an independent exhibition there that announced him as an Impressionist. At first, the critics and reviewers remained silent. Initially, the press seemed indifferent to the exhibition, sales were poor and Monet was bitterly disappointed, feeling that as the first, he was being used as an experiment

for Durand-Ruel and the other Impressionists. He wrote several letters to Durand-Ruel complaining of this, but more positive and sympathetic reviews

soon appeared. Some critics suggested that although his work was odd, one could become accustomed to it and even begin to see some value in it.

THE VILLAGE OF GIVERNY

In April 1883, Monet had to vacate the house in Poissy. He was not sorry, having never taken to the area, but he needed to find somewhere that would stimulate him as much as Argenteuil and Vétheuil had done. By the end of the month, he had found and moved into a house in a village called Giverny. Lying between Normandy and the Île-de-France on the right bank of the River Seine, it was 80km (50 miles) from Paris and the same distance the other way, from Rouen. A mile up the road was the village of Vernon, surrounded by beautiful and varied countryside. In 1883, the village of Giverny had 279 inhabitants. The move was only made possible by the generous financial assistance of Durand-Ruel.

Top: Haystacks, Lazy Sun, *1884. Monet creates an animated scene with strong contrasts of light and shade.*

Above: Bordighera, *1884. Intensifying his palette, he enthused about "this brilliance, this magical light".*

Others were even more supportive and an article in *La Vie Moderne* by Armand Silvestre praised the exhibition as a triumph. While it was not quite that, in hindsight, the exhibition can be seen as a turning point in Monet's fortunes.

SETTLING IN

Within days of moving in to the house in Giverny, Monet learned with great sadness of the death of Manet and he was a pallbearer at his friend's funeral. Returning to Giverny, he determined to make the most of his time and set about painting the surrounding area. Attached to the house was a garden surrounded by meadows, a railway and the River Ru, a small tributary of the River Epte, which flowed into the Seine. Monet spent several days painting on the water. He was charmed by the country surrounding Giverny but he also scouted for new landscapes.

That summer he also visited his brother Léon at Rouen and was joined there by Durand-Ruel and Pissarro. Durand-Ruel organized an exhibition of Impressionist painting in London to attract new buyers, but it was not particularly successful and toward the end of 1883, he commissioned Monet to paint some large decorative panels for his home in Paris. The decorations

kept Monet busy for some time, but during the last two weeks of December, he set off with Renoir to the South of France and Italy, searching for new sources of inspiration.

THE MEDITERRANEAN TRIP

After visiting Cézanne at Aix-en-Provence, the two artists moved on to Italy. In Renoir's words, the

Above: Rough Sea at Étretat, *1883. Étretat, with its bathing coves and steep cliffs had long been popular among artists, including Boudin, Corot and Courbet.*

Mediterranean inspired them to use beautiful colours. Monet was particularly enthralled by Bordighera and returned there alone the following January. He had written to Durand-Ruel: "I want to spend a month at Bordighera, one of the most beautiful spots we saw on our trip. I hope to bring you back a whole set of new things. But please don't tell anyone about this trip…I have always worked better alone, relying solely on my impressions…" Monet felt that he had found an earthly paradise in Bordighera and executed almost 50 paintings there.

During his second stay in Bordighera, from mid-January to mid-April 1884, Monet sent Alice letters declaring his love and describing his diligence. Inclined to be jealous of his long absences, she must have been reassured by Monet's letters. He was producing vast amounts of work in a relatively short time.

Left: Villas in Bordighera, *1884. This painting emits the warmth and golden light of the Mediterranean.*

THE GIVERNY STUDIO

Monet stayed in Bordighera from January to April 1884 before settling down in Giverny. During that time, he wrote affectionate letters to Alice, often describing his work – "I should like to paint orange and lemon trees standing against the blue sea."

From Italy, Monet warned Durand-Ruel that he was using a different palette to capture the light and atmosphere. "I will concentrate on the palm trees and the more exotic features… everything is shot with dove colours and the elusive blue of a flaming punch bowl." By the end of June, he had produced 22 canvases, which he brought back for Durand-Ruel. The dealer, however, could not buy all of the new paintings because he was about to open a gallery in New York.

THE FIRST STUDIO

On his return from Italy, Monet and Alice began creating a welcoming home at Giverny. He created a studio out of the barn in the west part of the house and finished all his paintings there.

In August 1884, he returned to Étretat with Alice and the children and repeatedly painted the cliffs and sea. Returning to Giverny, he worked in the new studio whenever he chose. He also began entertaining friends and other visitors in the studio, including Guy de Maupassant (1850–93) and Stéphane Mallarmé (1842–98).

THE ART DEALERS

Durand-Ruel was experiencing financial problems, which worried Monet enough to consider approaching other dealers. At the end of 1884, he spoke once more to Petit, the art dealer he worked with previously. Petit put Monet in an awkward position by offering him a place in his next annual *International Exhibition*, on the condition that no paintings belonging to Durand-Ruel would be included. Monet managed a compromise and took part in several of the *International Exhibitions* at Petit's Parisian gallery, but rather than leave the man who had provided for him for the last five years, he managed to share his work between the two dealers.

DEPARTING FROM IMPRESSIONISM

In the spring of 1886, at the invitation of the Secretary to the French Embassy in The Hague, Monet spent ten days painting in Holland, accompanied by Blanche Hoschedé. Fascinated by the fields of tulips, he produced five paintings there. Meanwhile, Pissarro had entreated him to take part in the Eighth Impressionist Exhibition, which was held in Paris between May and June 1886, but Monet declined. Although until then he had maintained that he was an Impressionist and the group's unofficial

Above: Woman with a Parasol turned to the Right, *1886. Monet painted two versions of this and significantly called them* Attempts at Figures in the Open Air.

leader, he realized that both he and the style were moving in separate directions. Georges Seurat (1859–91) and Cézanne were both experimenting with different ways of depicting colour and form and Monet needed to prove that he also had something new and worthwhile to offer.

Below: Self-Portrait with a Beret, *1886. Monet painted his first self-portrait when he was 46.*

Above: Villas at Bordighera, Italy, *1884. Monet found the Italian Riviera to be one of the most beautiful places he had visited.*

MEETING GEFFROY AND CLEMENCEAU

That autumn, Monet visited the Atlantic for the first time, at Belle Ile off the coast of Brittany. He worked in all weathers, covering his canvases with the pounding waves hitting the rocks, once again eliminating all forms of humanity from them. He worked from just a few sites, capturing similar views in changing conditions. While painting there, he met the art critic Gustave Geffroy (1855–1926) who wrote for the radical newspaper *La Justice* and who admired his work. From then on, Geffroy became one of Monet's closest friends and he introduced him to another supportive friend who was also his editor, and who was to be the future Prime Minister of France, Georges Clemenceau (1841–1929).

That summer he painted his first self-portrait. Although his face looks at the viewer with a concerned expression, it seems that this painting was simply a vehicle for Monet to practise new skills and to manipulate both the paint and his abilities as a draughtsman, not a new direction for his work. He continued painting figures

that summer, in the open air, this time using Suzanne Hoschedé as his model. In a similar pose to Camille's in the painting *Woman with a Parasol* of 1876, Suzanne, then aged 18, stood on a hill, holding a parasol and Monet painted the effects of the weather around her rather than a detailed likeness of her. These were some of his last large-scale figure paintings.

Right: The Rocks at Belle Île, *1886. Monet captured the melancholy atmosphere in the dark blue rocks.*

CHANGE IN FORTUNES

In 1886, Monet made his American debut at the first Impressionist exhibition in New York organized by Durand-Ruel. The show attracted huge crowds, many of his paintings were sold, and the press was unanimously favourable.

Although Monet's paintings were well received in the United States of America, Monet had no desire to travel there, preferring to work from Giverny.

GOOD REVIEWS
From late 1886 to early 1887, Monet left Giverny as little as possible. Even during the summer of 1887, he spent most of his time there, painting the surroundings and his family.

In the sixth *International Exhibition* at Petit's gallery in the spring of 1887, Monet exhibited eight of the paintings he had produced at Belle Île the year before and most of the reviews about the works were favourable. The novelist Joris-Karl Huysmans for example, wrote that Monet was "the most significant landscape painter of modern times", while Alfred de Lostalot said his paintings "had the power to silence the critics". Geffroy in particular praised the work and also gave an account of Monet's working methods that he had witnessed directly at Belle Île.

That year, Monet returned to London for the first time since 1871 and spent a fortnight there with his friend Whistler. Monet agreed to promote Whistler in Paris and in reciprocation Whistler did the same for Monet in London. Whistler was

Above: Antibes, *1888. The effects of the mistral can be seen in the light touches where the sun glints on the water.*

exhibiting with the Society of British Artists and introduced Monet as an honourable member. Monet helped him hold an exhibition of his watercolours and pastels in Petit's gallery in Paris.

THEO VAN GOGH
Despite his worry that new artists might overtake him, Monet's work in fact attracted the admiration of younger artists. Theo van Gogh (1857–91) an art dealer in Paris visited him in his studio at Giverny. Envious, his brother Vincent wrote to Theo, "You'll see some beautiful things at Monet's." But instead of becoming arrogant because younger artists found him inspirational, Monet worried that he would not be able to keep up the standards that were expected of him. On behalf of the

Left: Haystack at Giverny, *1886. This was a precursor of the many haystack paintings that Monet produced in 1893.*

Above: In the Woods at Giverny: Blanche Hoschedé at her Easel with Suzanne Hoschedé Reading, *1887.*

Below: Field of Yellow Irises at Giverny, *1887. Monet painted the landscape of Giverny with a sense of liberty and purpose.*

KEEPING UP WITH COMPETITION

Although Monet was achieving approval in several quarters now, he was concerned that his new-found popularity would not last long in the light of the growing competition there was from younger artists. He told Alice, "One has to do everything." He decided to go back to the South of France, this time to Antibes and Juan-les-Pins where he could once again concentrate on the brilliant light of the Mediterranean. Yet while there, he still alternated between hope and despair. He wrote that he believed he was not progressing and that he could not finish anything. As his moods changed, so did the emotion in his letters to Alice, "This is the third day on which I haven't been able to paint!" A few days later he wrote again, "I'm working like a madman."

Goupil Gallery, Theo bought ten of the Antibes paintings for 11,900 francs and agreed to pay Monet 50 per cent of the resale profit. He exhibited the paintings privately at 19 boulevard Montmartre and there was a steady flow of eminent visitors, including Maupassant, Prince Eugene of Sweden and Mallarmé, who commented, "Ah yes, as poor Édouard [Manet] always used to say, Monet is a genius." Vincent van Gogh wrote to Theo, "Who will be to figure painting what Monet is to landscape?"

PAINTING LIGHT AND WEATHER

In 1889, Paris opened its doors with the Exposition Universelle, which was intended to exhibit France's glory and achievements to the whole world. Reviews about Monet's work were still mixed. Undaunted, he started the first series paintings in different lights and varying weather conditions.

Monet worked for three months on his Creuse Valley series so that he could exhibit them at the Exposition.

MORE REVIEWS

Opinions about Monet's work were still divided. The painter Pierre-Georges Jeanniot (1848–1934) reported in the *Cravache Parisienne* that Monet did not have "what one could call a studio", and that he never retouched his work. Both of these observations were incorrect: Monet worked in his studio at Giverny and never let a painting go before he had finished it in the studio. In actual fact, Jeanniot had visited the studio, but described it as a "sort of barn" where Monet piled up his paintings. Jeanniot also accompanied Monet on a painting expedition around Giverny and described his method of work as "he starts painting after a few charcoal outlines, wielding his long paintbrushes with surprising agility and assurance of line: his landscape is quickly fleshed out and could, at a pinch, be left unchanged after the first session."

Another artist, Félix Fénéon (1861–1944) wrote in *Le Revue Indépendante* that Monet had no contemplation or analysis in him. He painted with excessive technical bravura and brilliant vulgarity. He said

the work was not the art of a refined man. With such an assortment of assessments, it is no wonder that Monet spent so much time doubting his abilities and striving to achieve something different.

Above: Valley of the Creuse (Sunlight Effect), *1889. This was one of 14 Creuse paintings at the Monet–Rodin exhibition.*

Below: The Grande Creuse at Pont de Vervy, *1889. Monet's Creuse Valley paintings concentrated on land and water.*

THE EXPOSITION UNIVERSELLE

Universal exhibitions were held in Paris every 11 years from the mid-19th century. The 1889 Exposition Universelle was dominated by the Eiffel Tower, which served as the entrance to the fair. Built on the Champ de Mars, the site of the earlier Paris *Exposition Universelle* of 1867, it was the largest interior space in the world at the time and was filled with a spectacular display of exhibits. Three of Monet's paintings were exhibited at the *Centennial of French Art*, which opened in May 1889 to mark the Exposition.

REPETITION

Increasingly, Monet painted the same views in different light and weather effects. In Antibes and Juan-les-Pins for instance, he painted almost 40 canvases of about six views. Aware of the risk of being labelled repetitive or unimaginative, he tried to create something different in each work. In Normandy and Brittany this was manageable because of the variable weather and landscape, but in the South of France, the climate and scenery were noticeably consistent. "I must guard against repeating myself," he told Alice. His Impressionist friends were critical of the paintings. Pissarro thought they did not represent highly developed art, Renoir considered them retrograde and Degas believed they were made for the commercial market.

THE CREUSE VALLEY

In February 1889, Monet went with Geffroy to stay with the poet Maurice Rollinat (1846–1903) in Fresselines in the Creuse Valley. Captivated by the countryside, Monet spent three months there. Unfortunately, bad weather besieged him however. He wrote to Alice, "I am utterly miserable, almost discouraged and so tired that I am almost ill…I have never been so unlucky with the weather!" Persistent rain prevented him from venturing out until the first spring buds began appearing on the trees, but rather than abandon his plans, he paid two farm hands to remove the buds from an oak tree and he continued painting the 'winter' tree.

THE RODIN EXHIBITION

That June, he shared a large exhibition in Paris with his friend, the sculptor Auguste Rodin (1840–1917) at Petit's gallery. He included 14 of his Creuse Valley paintings and 130 other works, alongside sculptures by Rodin who had already received official recognition. The exhibition was a resounding success.

Above: Effect of Spring, Giverny, *1890. Several trees set against an azure sky act as a foil for the bright foreground.*

Left: The Seine at Port-Villez, *c.1890. Many of Monet's landscapes from this time featured only essential elements.*

HAYSTACKS AND POPLARS

With the success of the Creuse Valley paintings, Monet pushed the idea of series paintings a step further. He began painting the same motif, over and over again, in all lights and weathers, exploring the consequences of changing atmospheric effects.

Whatever motif he chose, colour and light became the subject. Never had shadows and highlights been so vibrant.

PROGRESSION

Gradually, objects in Monet's landscapes became less significant as he committed himself to depicting mood and ambience. In a letter to Geffroy in October 1890, he wrote: "I am hard at work; I am adamant about doing a series of different effects, but at this time of the year the sun sets so quickly that I can't follow it…I am becoming so slow in my work that it exasperates me. The further I go, the more I see that it is necessary to work a great deal in order to achieve what I am looking for…I am more and more passionate about the need to convey what I feel."

For the previous couple of years, he worked this way, but during 1890, he rarely painted single pictures, preferring to produce several depictions of one scene. He said that when we first look at a view, we bring preconceptions and opinions to it, but he was trying to portray what he saw without any of

that, simply capturing the colours and shapes. This was a natural progression from what he had been painting for years already, only by the end of the 19th century, he intensified it.

HAYSTACKS

In 1890 and 1891, he worked on a series of paintings of haystacks from fields near his house in Giverny. Notable

Above: Haystacks in the Sun, Morning Effect, 1891. *Exploring the effects of light, weather and atmosphere, Monet painted the same view over and again. Here an early morning moment has been captured with soft, opalescent colours.*

for their mediocrity, although he had painted them earlier, the haystacks were used as a neutral motif for light and atmospheric effects. He painted over 20 haystack canvases, hardly varying the viewpoint and recording his perceptions of colour and mood during a short period of time. He called his impressions of light and atmosphere the *enveloppe,* which meant the atmospheric effects due to the time of day, the weather and the seasons.

By the spring of 1891 he had executed 25 paintings of the haystacks; from these he chose 15 to be included in an exhibition of 22 works at Durand-Ruel's gallery in May 1891. He told one visitor to the show, "For me, a landscape does not exist in its own

Left: Haystacks at Sunset, Frosty Weather, 1891. *Monet captured the frosty cool hues in this picture.*

right, since its appearance changes at every moment; but its surroundings bring it to life, through the air and the light, which continually vary…"

The exhibition was a critical and financial success. Almost every haystack canvas was sold within the year, once again with the majority being bought by American collectors. A letter from Pissarro to his son verified the popularity of the paintings. In it, he said, "People want only Monets, it seems he can't paint enough to go round…. Everything he does goes straight to America at prices of four, five and six thousand francs." For the first time in several years, Pissarro was also full of praise for his friend's latest efforts. At the exhibition he declared, "These paintings seem to me very luminous, undoubtedly the work of a master."

THE TREE OF LIBERTY

In the spring of 1891, Monet began painting a series of poplar trees that lined the River Epte, a few miles out of Giverny at the village of Lamas. The trees, planted in a line equidistant from each other, were intended to be felled

Above: Poplars on the Epte, c.1891. *The line of poplar trees curve around the Epte under sunlight, and the leaves and water flicker with reflections and highlights.*

and sold as timber, but Monet made a deal with the timber merchant so that they would be left standing for a few more months. Poplars had a special meaning for the French – they had been selected as the 'tree of liberty' during the Revolution, so Monet was also possibly choosing them for patriotic reasons. Retaining compositional simplicity, he produced more than 20 paintings of the poplars with variations in lighting according to weather and seasons. All his poplar canvases are on a vertical or portrait format. Exhibited in an exhibition at Durand-Ruel's gallery the next spring, the paintings were an instant success.

Left: Poplars, 1891. *Using a limited palette and flickering brushstrokes, he has created what appears like a transitory sketch.*

ROUEN CATHEDRAL

Monet's series paintings marked a turning point in his work. After the success of his haystacks series in 1890–91, he continued to exploit the idea of painting the same motif under different light and atmospheric conditions.

Some depressing events occurred in 1890. In July, Monet learned of Van Gogh's suicide, which was followed in October by his brother Theo's breakdown. Ernest Hoschedé had been suffering for some time from violent pains in his legs. This was diagnosed as gout and had been treated, but from November, the condition worsened.

AN UNCANNY COINCIDENCE

With his health deteriorating rapidly, Hoschedé moved to a room in Paris, where he became bedridden. He moved into 45 rue Laffitte – the address of Monet's birth, although the street had been renumbered since 1840, so it was not the same building. Alice, duty-bound to help her husband of ten years, moved in to care for him. She nursed him tirelessly – as she had

attended Camille in her last days – however, after nearly a week, Hoschedé died. Monet paid for his funeral, which was conducted where he had been baptized over 50 years previously, at the church of Notre-Dame-de-Lorette.

THE COLOURFUL CATHEDRAL

In early February 1892, Monet went to stay with Léon in Rouen. He determined to paint a series of pictures of Rouen Cathedral, a Gothic cathedral that, until about ten years previously, had been the tallest building in the world. It was also famous for containing the heart of Richard the Lionheart.

Deciding that he spent too much time chatting with his brother, Monet moved into a room above a clothing shop, overlooking the medieval place de la Cathédrale. It gave him a direct and

clear view of the building, but he was not popular because ladies purchasing from the shop below used the room that Monet was in to try on clothes. Even though he had his back to the room and spent the entire time looking out of the window, the women were not comfortable and complained. Monet was resolute and continued, ignoring them and their grievances. He wanted to capture atmospheric effects of light against an architectural structure rather than a natural one. Changing his canvas almost every half an hour, he carefully observed the play of light and shade on the west façade of the cathedral, capturing the embellished surface. Over two sessions, Monet ended up producing more than 30 canvases of Rouen Cathedral from three slightly different angles between

Above: Rouen Cathedral at the End of the Day, Sunlight Effect, *1892–93. Most of Monet's Rouen Cathedral paintings are dated 1894, but he painted them over two sessions, in early 1892 and 1893.*

Above: Rouen Cathedral at Sunset, *1894. The cathedral was simply a backdrop for Monet's creative research. He used it to see how shapes change as shifting sunlight creates different effects.*

Above: Rouen Cathedral, West Portal, Grey Weather, *1894. Monet's technique was to build up textures with thick layers of paint to create the impression of stonework in relief.*

1892 and 1894, each showing a remarkable difference in colour and tone. He wrote to Alice of the difficulties of the work he was trying to do and of his obsession with it: "I am worn out, I give up and what's more, something that never happens to me, I couldn't sleep for nightmares: the cathedral was collapsing on me, it was blue or pink or yellow." In another letter, he wrote to her, "This devil of a cathedral, how hard it is to paint!" Still, he was pleased with the outcome and 20 of the canvases were included in an exhibition of his recent works at Durand-Ruel's gallery in May 1895.

MARRYING ALICE

Monet returned to Giverny in April 1892. He continued teaching Blanche to paint, but was especially keen to discuss the forthcoming marriage of Alice's other daughter Suzanne, to an American

Above: Blanche Hoschedé Painting, *1892. Monet had been teaching Blanche to paint for some time as she was fascinated by her stepfather's work. The artist in the background is probably Sargent; Suzanne is looking over his shoulder.*

painter Theodore Butler (1861–1936). Monet did not approve of the match, because they did not know anything about Butler's family and because he was an artist! Eventually he accepted Butler into the family, but this was one of several instances that showed Monet's dislike of disruptions to the family set-up. Around mid-July, he wrote to tell Durand-Ruel that the marriage would be taking place – after his own to Alice. On 16 July, he and Alice married in Giverny and he gave his stepdaughter away at her own nuptials four days later. After 12 years of living together, the gossip about Monet and Alice's domestic arrangements subsided.

PLANS FOR GIVERNY

With the help of a loan from Durand-Ruel in 1890, Monet was able to buy the house in Giverny. After the house came the purchase of a plot of land adjoining the bottom of the garden. Three years later, Durand-Ruel put on an exhibition of prints by Utamaro (c.1753–1806) and Hiroshige (1797–1858), prominent Japanese artists. Meeting there, Monet and Pissarro were both impressed by the compositions and designs, but Monet in particular was inspired by the ideas of still water, exotic plants and Japanese bridges. The piece of land he had just bought at the end of the garden became a new project – a Japanese-style garden.

ENTERTAINING AT GIVERNY

In 1893, Alice became ill and Monet spent a lot of time at Giverny as she recuperated, playing host to many visitors. He took the opportunity to oversee his garden and pond, which were in the process of being built on his newly acquired land.

In 1891, Monet received a visit from a Japanese gardener and in 1893, he obtained permission to divert part of the River Ru to make a pool for water plants.

DEVELOPMENTS AT HOME

Organizing the design of his garden became another of Monet's passions. With his painter's eye, he selected the flowers and other plants in different proportions and colour combinations. He planned the walkways and trellises, which flowers would bloom in certain months and which would bloom at other times, making sure that the colours he surrounded himself with were those he wished to paint at any given time. He also supervised the construction of three greenhouses as well as the digging of the pond, which he filled with white water lilies. He had the house painted pink with green shutters and the dining room, where he frequently entertained guests, bright yellow. Hundreds of Japanese prints covered the walls.

FINANCIAL SECURITY AND FRIENDS

For the first time, Monet was financially comfortable. His paintings were now selling at high prices and he had become extremely well known. Even the promise of younger painters, such as the late Van Gogh and Paul Gauguin (1848–1903) who boldly experimented with colour, did not detract from his popularity and success. Yet even with such a positive improvement in his circumstances, he was soon plunged into depression when his friends and patrons, Caillebotte and de Bellio died tragically young, and he also heard that Amand Gautier, who had once advised him, had also passed away.

In the autumn of 1894, several friends paid him visits at Giverny. These included Mary Cassatt, Cézanne, Rodin, Clemenceau, Renoir, Sisley, Pissarro, Geffroy and the writer Octave Mirbeau (1848–1917). All guests were sure of a warm and generous welcome at the Monets. By then, his paintings sold for

THE WORLD FAIR IN CHICAGO

To celebrate the 400th anniversary of the discovery by Christopher Columbus of the New World, in 1893, the World's Columbian Exposition was held in Chicago. Among other exhibits, it featured an Art Palace where the French Impressionists were given their own special section. A number of Monet's paintings were exhibited.

an average of 12,000 francs, in comparison to the typical 184 francs of 20 years previously. He was delighted to be able to entertain them all lavishly, but his art nonetheless came before everything. Geffroy observed: "Suddenly Monet grabbed his palette and brushes. 'The sun is out again,' he said, but at that moment he was the only one who knew it. Look as we might, we still saw nothing."

Above: Monet's Garden at Giverny, c.1880. Capturing his garden in rich and brilliant colours, Monet painted his flowers over and again.

Left: The garden and atelier of Monet's house, 2004. In later life, Giverny was his most important source of inspiration.

NORWEGIAN SNOW SCENES

Unlike the harsh winters Monet had experienced at Vétheuil, his first few at Giverny were fairly mild, which did not give him the breadth of subjects and themes he wanted to explore. With snow scenes in mind and a change of scene needed, in the spring of 1895 he went to Norway to visit his stepson Jacques Hoschedé. In search of subject matter, he travelled around the Christiania region (now Oslo). After a period of depression, he eventually settled in a small village called Bjørnegaard where he stayed in an artist's commune. From there he painted landscapes of the fjords and houses nestled in the snow in the surrounding area, in particular exploring the colour effects of light and shadow on snow and ice. "Nowhere are there such beautiful effects as here. I mean

Above: Mount Kolsaas, Norway, *1895.*
Monet's brushstrokes suggest snow and fir
trees without committing to detail.

effects of snow which are absolutely stunning, but unbelievably difficult…", he wrote to Blanche. He also executed 13 paintings of Mount Kolsaas, which reminded him of the Japanese prints he admired of Mount Fujiyama.

He painted in Bjørnegaard until it began to thaw and at the end of March travelled back to Christiania. The work he produced there is raw and sketchy with an almost unfinished air. He wrote of them that they would "be neither impressions nor very finished paintings." At Christiania, Prince Eugene of Sweden went specifically to meet Monet, to admire his work. The last time he had seen Monet's work was in 1887 at the Goupil Gallery in rue de Montmartre. Some days later, at the beginning of April, Monet returned to Giverny. Immediately he got home, he wrote to Durand-Ruel, "I am not too unhappy with the things I've brought back."

Left: Norway, Red Houses at Bjørnegaard, *1895. The serenity of this light-dappled view is enhanced by the limited palette and a simple composition, reminiscent of the Japanese style.*

THE SEINE SERIES

After his exhibition at Durand-Ruel's gallery in May 1895, Monet painted few new works for several months. His time was taken up with finishing the Norwegian paintings in his studio and organizing the building of his garden.

Although his garden was taking shape in 1895, Monet rarely painted it until the plants were more mature and the foliage had spread. During that year, he also visited two retrospective exhibitions for Corot and Cézanne. As Corot was one of his first role models and Cézanne's paintings showed exploration of one theme over and again, Monet was possibly inspired to return to subjects and locations that he had previously visited and to explore his ideas in further depth.

RETURN TO THE SEA

Early in 1896, he returned to the Normandy coast locations of Pourville, Varengeville and Dieppe, taking with him sketchbooks he had completed there in 1882. He wrote to Durand-Ruel's son Joseph, who had joined the business, "I needed to see the sea again and am delighted to see again so many things that I did 15 years ago." He painted a number of seascapes from

Above: Branch of the Seine near Giverny, *1897. In this series, Monet's colour range is more limited than in previous works.*

Below: The Cliffs near Dieppe, *1897. Monet revisited the Normandy coast, which he had not seen for 15 years.*

just a few locations and became even more involved in the weather and atmospheric effects.

SUMMER ON THE SEINE

Monet always treated the sea as a subject in itself, while rivers, ponds and lakes were usually included in his works solely for their reflective qualities. By the end of the 19th century, however, they had become some of his preferred subjects for exploring light and colour. During the spring and summer of 1897, he began his *Morning on the Seine* series, in which he spent most days travelling around the rivers Seine and Epte, from early dawn throughout the morning, painting wispy effects of early morning mists smudging the shapes of the trees and banks. Sometimes starting out at 3.30 a.m., he worked from his studio boat, studying

THE DREYFUS AFFAIR

Between 1894 and 1906, the Dreyfus Affair precipitated a national conflict in France. Alfred Dreyfus (1859–1935) was a young French army officer of Jewish heritage. In 1894, it was discovered that some confidential information, was being passed to the Germans. Dreyfus, being one of the few Jews in the army, was arrested. He was sentenced to life imprisonment and incarcerated in solitary confinement at Devil's Island in French Guyana. The following year, the real traitor was found, but Dreyfus remained in prison.

Pissarro and Zola were among many artists and writers who believed in his innocence and Zola wrote a letter to the newspaper *L'Aurore* in 1898; it became known as 'J'accuse' (I accuse), calling for justice. Zola was then convicted of libel. Monet signed a manifesto in support of Dreyfus. Zola's letter provoked interest in the case and in 1899, Dreyfus was pardoned and freed. The effect of the affair was so damaging, however, that it helped to bring about the demise of the Impressionist movement.

Above: Chrysanthemums, *1897. Monet has built up pattern and rhythm across the canvas for this 'snapshot' image.*

light conditions and how the sun changes the colours and appearance of trees, skies and the river. He also sought compositions that exploited a balance of solid masses with air and light. As with his previous series paintings, he changed his canvases

frequently as the light changed and by the end of the year had produced a series of 30 pictures. He remained full of self-doubt about his abilities to paint things quickly and well and to recreate the effects that he saw so clearly.

Below: The Seine at Giverny, Morning Mists, *1897. Morning mist obscures details, creating a calm and quiet effect.*

Below: Morning on the Seine near Giverny, *1897. Monet began 14 canvases of this view simultaneously.*

FAMILY LIFE AND EXHIBITIONS

In 1897, there was much upheaval in the Monet family. Monet's brother Léon, who had been a widower for two years, remarried a much younger woman and Jean Monet began talking of marrying his stepsister Blanche Hoschedé.

Monet did not think that his son Jean marrying Blanche was a good idea, but Alice overruled him and the wedding took place. At once, his stepdaughter, assistant and pupil, became his daughter-in-law too. Jean and Blanche decided to move to Rouen, where Jean would work for his uncle Léon.

EN FAMILLE

Meanwhile, Monet felt a strong feeling of nostalgia for the past and returned to locations he had worked at before. In 1896 and 1897 he worked at Pourville and Varengeville, painting the whole time outdoors, but retouching the canvases in his studio later. By then

his garden was finished and he spent time enjoying it with his family. Jean-Pierre Hoschedé later described him as a gourmet and not a glutton and that while he would only eat top quality food and drink fine wine, he never over-indulged. Jean-Pierre described a cosy image of family life at the Monet household, with Monet taking part in some of the cooking.

A VISIT FROM A JOURNALIST

In August 1897, journalist Maurice Guillemot (1859–1931) who was writing for *La Revue Illustrée* visited Monet at Giverny in order to write an account of his working day. He joined

Monet on one of his Seine painting trips and described how they left at 3.30 a.m.; walked to the point where the River Epte met the Seine, climbed into a boat and rowed to Monet's floating studio boat. A garden worker helped to unpack several canvases, which were numbered and in packages of two. Monet wanted Guillemot's readers to know his working methods and that his paintings depicting

Below: The House at Douanier, Pink Effect, 1897. *Once used by military officers to enforce taxes on goods shipped by sea, this small house was no longer in use by the time Monet painted it.*

Above: Banks of the Seine at Vernon, *1897. The canvas has greens and yellows in the foreground corner and muted blues in the distance.*

CAILLEBOTTE'S BEQUEST

Caillebotte had been particularly generous toward his friends and fellow artists during his life. Characteristically philanthropic, he had left a legacy of paintings for the State. These included 14 works by Monet, 19 by Pissarro, 10 by Renoir and many others by Sisley, Degas, Cézanne and Manet. With foresight, Caillebotte requested that an exhibition of the paintings be held at the Musée du Luxembourg, where the work of living artists was shown and later transferred to the Louvre. There was controversy over this as many Salon officials opposed the idea of showing these radical artists works to the public from a conventional platform. Eventually, on 7 February 1897, the Caillebotte bequest was hung in an extension of the Musée du Louvre. Despite the trepidation of the bureaucrats, the exhibition proved popular.

mornings on the Seine actually took many long hours of work and effort. In the ensuing article, Guillemot also mentioned Monet's fascination with his pond and a couple of huge canvases he had executed in his Giverny studio.

SUCCESSFUL AND FREQUENT EXHIBITIONS

By the 1890s, communication was better than ever before, largely due to railways, better postal services, advances in photography and more efficient printing. In various capital cities, regular international exhibitions of contemporary art were held and were well received, giving artists far greater opportunities to become known abroad than ever before. During the 1890s, for instance, Impressionist exhibitions were held in Brussels, Stockholm, Venice, Florence and Vienna.

All the artists included in the exhibitions achieved significant prestige around Europe. In 1898, Durand-Ruel held Impressionist exhibitions in Munich and Berlin. On 8 January, works by Monet and Manet were also included in an exhibition at the South London Art Gallery and in May, Durand-Ruel held an exhibition in his Paris gallery of works by Monet, Renoir, Pissarro and Sisley. The following month, another exhibition at Durand-Ruel's, this time of recent work by Pissarro, included several of Monet's paintings.

Simultaneously, Monet enjoyed another successful exhibition at Petit's gallery, while in July in London, the International Society of Artists held an exhibition of Impressionism organized by Whistler.

Monet owed a lot to the support of Durand-Ruel, who steadfastly promoted the Impressionists, despite criticism from the official Salon. His persistence finally led to success after he opened galleries around the world.

Below: The Shore, *1897. In this painting, Monet seems to have been attracted to the atmospheric effects of light and air.*

PERSONAL TRAGEDY

As Monet approached 60, he was financially secure and respected. In May 1899, Monet, Pissarro, Renoir and Rodin were included in an exhibition of the International Society of Artists at the New Gallery in London. His personal life suffered a terrible setback, however.

With the development of his series paintings, particularly the latest Seine series, views differed on Monet's achievement. Some critics declared that Monet's art was declining. Others felt he had moved too far away from Impressionism and only a few anticipated the ideas he had in mind for the next phase of his art. Everyone, it seems, had an opinion about his current and forthcoming work. Because Guillemot and Geffroy had visited Giverny, they were unique among his reviewers who knew about the size and scope of his pond. A few other artist friends also knew of the garden and pond and possibly a little of his future plans for using his garden as a subject, although no one knew quite what he intended. Some knew him well enough to recognize that something important was planned.

REPUTATION

In 1899, following the precedent that had been set in recent years, several more exhibitions were arranged. In Russia, the Imperial Society for the Encouragement of the Arts held an

exhibition of French art that included several works by Monet, and in the U.S.A., solo exhibitions for him were organized in New York and Boston.

As a direct result of all this exposure, Monet's reputation was rapidly increasing throughout Europe and the U.S.A.

Left: Alice Monet, Nadar (Gaspard Felix Tournachon), 1899, silver print, black and white photograph.

Above: Suzanne, c.1885. This sensitive pastel rendition captures her as a thoughtful young girl.

Above: Ice at Bennecourt, 1898. Using purples, greens and blues, Monet has created an air of mystery in this picture.

SORROW

In the midst of his success and schemes for the future, once again, sadness touched him. In 1898, his friend Mallarmé died and Alfred Sisley, who he had met at Gleyre's studio 37 years before, developed cancer of the throat. In January 1899, Sisley called Monet to his home. Still struggling for recognition, Sisley implored Monet to help his family after his death. Within days he was

Above: Waterloo Bridge, c.1899 (pastel on paper), painted from the Savoy.

dead and later that year, Monet organized a posthumous exhibition of his work at Petit's gallery to raise money for his family.

Meanwhile, further sorrow was ahead; Alice's daughter Suzanne had symptoms of paralysis. As she was only 30 years old, the illness was not considered to be life threatening. Yet within a couple of days she was dead. Alice's grief was overwhelming and she never stopped mourning her daughter. Naturally, this also affected Monet. He had been very fond of his stepdaughter and it was a strain to observe his wife

suffering such acute and persistent depression. For once, however, he was determined to be strong in order to help cheer up those he loved.

HELPING SISLEY'S FAMILY

The money raised for the exhibition at Petit's gallery that included works by Sisley and Monet helped Sisley's family. Another exhibition held by Durand-Ruel with works by Monet, Sisley, Renoir and Pissarro, also helped them.

LONDON

Partly to try and brighten Alice's spirits, partly to visit Michel who was living there and partly to re-examine the River Thames, in September 1899 Monet and Alice travelled to London. Michel Monet had been there since the spring and his father and stepmother wanted to inspect his lodgings. Once there, Monet set up his easel on his balcony on the fifth floor of the Savoy Hotel and painted the view.

THE JAPANESE BRIDGE

For most of his artistic life, Monet had acknowledged the admiration he held for Japanese art and design. He used the influence in his art and had made known for some time, his desire to create a Japanese style garden at Giverny.

Monet's scheme for his garden included a bridge and a pond in Japanese style, with Japanese bamboo and peonies.

INSPIRATION AND REFLECTION

Monet's initial idea to have the bridge built was possibly simply to paint its reflection on the pond. Hiroshige, whose work Monet had seen at Durand-Ruel's exhibition, had created a print of a Japanese bridge. Its proportions resemble Monet's bridge and the contrasts between the solidity of the structure with the delicacy of the flowers surrounding it are also remarkably similar.

In the middle months of 1899, Monet began working on his first paintings of his Japanese bridge. Although not many were aware of it at the time, these paintings were the

result of years of contemplation and deliberation about what he would do with his water garden and how he would compose his pictures of it. The wooden bridge was made to his design

Below: Footbridge over River with Wisteria in Foreground in Full Bloom, *Ando or Utagawa Hiroshige, (1797–1858), 1856, colour woodblock print. This print represents a shrine and garden.*

EAST MEETS WEST

Monet's garden was in two parts, on either side of the road. The flower garden in front of the house was called Clos Normand and the Japanese-inspired water garden was created across the road. The two parts complement each other, with their Western and Eastern influences. The flower garden was constructed geometrically and filled with flowers, plants, bushes and trees that reminded Monet of gardens he had seen and admired in both Normandy and in Britain. The water garden was mysterious and exotic, abundant with Eastern plants, including bamboo, gingko and Japanese fruit trees. When it was first created, the pond covered approximately 1,000 square metres (10,764 sq ft), surrounded by trailing, spreading flowers, trees and bushes.

Above: The Water Lily Pond: Harmony in Green, *1899. This version of one of Monet's favourite motifs is tranquil and serene.*

Top right: White Water Lilies, *1899. The lilies are enhanced by the contrasts of the water and leaves surrounding them.*

Above: Water Lilies and Japanese Bridge, *1899. The reflections of the sky highlight the lush foliage and arch of the bridge.*

and during the summer of 1899, he spent weeks painting several canvases of it and the lily pond.

His reasons for working there that summer were twofold. He wished to remain close to Alice in her grief-stricken state and he also wanted to fulfil an ambition of painting the bridge and lilies. He had first painted water lilies in a series of studies in 1897, but in 1899 he produced 18 canvases of them under the Japanese bridge. He used the large, sweeping arc of the bridge as a foil for the fragile lilies beneath, contrasting colour, line and shape and dividing the images into two halves; the lower part filled with water and the upper half filled with sky. The enclosed space gives each painting an overall impression of calm and serenity.

MUTUAL FASCINATION

Cézanne was one of the many artists who visited Giverny and worked there. Monet and Cézanne admired each other greatly and they had a common interest in their series paintings. Monet was fascinated by the methods Cézanne used in his series of paintings of Aix-en-Provence and his paintings of bridges.

In some ways the two artists had similarities, while in others, they were opposites. Both often used small, broken brushstrokes and colourful palettes, both painted motifs repeatedly that were familiar to them and both moved away from traditional elements of painting. On the other hand, Monet sought the ephemeral effects of light while Cézanne focused on solid form and structure. Cézanne allegedly said, "Monet is just an eye – but God, what an eye!" When the estate of Victor Chocquet was to be auctioned in 1899, Monet went even further to promote his friend. He wrote to a potential purchaser, asking him to buy a painting by Cézanne, even though 13 of his own works were in the auction.

A SECOND STUDIO

While Monet was working on his Japanese bridge series, he was also having a second studio built close to his house. This was a large two-storey building constructed to the left of the garden, in front of the greenhouses. The ground floor was used as storage and as a gardeners' room while on the first floor was a huge square room, well lit with large bay windows and skylights. It was spacious enough for Monet to work in and also to store many of his works. He later had a garage added, when he became interested in cars and turned his first studio into a sitting room, study and gallery for his private collection of paintings. He had a dark room for photography and two extra bedrooms. As his work grew larger, other additions were completed by 1916 to give him more space. Special easels held his massive later works and a sofa, on which to study and contemplate his work in progress.

LONDON

The Thames held a fascination for Monet. Since his first visit in 1870, he had been interested in the mysterious London light. In 1899, it seemed that the time was right to return and spend some time painting there.

As well as painting views of the Thames, Monet intended to visit his son Michel, who was studying English in London.

THE SAVOY HOTEL

After five years and vast sums of money spent, the Savoy Hotel opened on the Strand in 1889. As London's first hotel to have electric lighting, from the moment the hotel doors were opened to the public, it was deemed the epitome of style and luxury, featuring 70 private baths and handmade beds. It also boasted magnificent views of the River Thames and became the venue for various extravagant parties.

Below: Waterloo Bridge, Cloudy Day, 1900. Monet built up his London series, which have an atmospheric mood.

In February 1896, Whistler travelled to London from Paris for medical treatment for his wife, who was fatally ill. They took rooms overlooking the Thames in the Savoy and Whistler sat with his wife while drawing the view from either the window or the balcony. Although she died that spring, Whistler remembered their time at the Savoy fondly. Three years later, he suggested it to Monet who booked a suite on the fifth floor for himself and Alice. The views from their windows included Charing Cross Bridge, Waterloo Bridge and the Houses of Parliament.

MONET'S VIEWS AND ROUTINE

The five canvases Monet painted in 1899 focused on the River Thames. The architecture appeared as indeterminate as the smoke, fog and mist, with no strong outlines or tones to differentiate them dramatically. By the end of October 1899, he and Alice returned to Giverny, but within three months, Monet had returned alone to carry on painting his London views. He returned again in December of 1901, always staying in the same rooms in the Savoy on the fifth floor. During those three visits, he produced over 100 paintings, including 42 of Waterloo Bridge, 35 of Charing Cross Bridge and 20 of the Houses of Parliament. He also produced about 20 pastels. His routine was extremely organized. Throughout the morning and after lunch, he worked at his window in the Savoy, painting either the Charing Cross or Waterloo bridges. Later in the

THE 1900 EXPOSITION UNIVERSELLE

From 15 April to 12 November 1900 in Paris, the Exposition Universelle was held to celebrate the achievements of the past century and to welcome the next. The Grand Palais and the Petit Palais were built in place of the Palais de l'Industrie and 14 of Monet's paintings were displayed in an exhibition. Several new buildings were constructed; including the Gare de Lyon, the Gare d'Orsay and the Pont Alexandre III. The first track of the Paris Metro was also laid. Another feature of the Exposition was the Second (Modern) Olympic Games, which took place over five months.

Above right: Waterloo Bridge, *1900. Selecting contemporary motifs for the first time in 20 years, Monet relished the chance to explore the juxtaposition of urban development with natural phenomena.*

Right: Study of Waterloo Bridge At Dusk, *1903.*

afternoon, he crossed the river to St Thomas' Hospital and painted the Houses of Parliament. The interplay of light on the river and buildings was intensified by his choppy brushmarks. Although his works give the impression of being painted almost as quickly as the light effects he captured, they were painted over months – he took them back and forth to England and France and worked on them in both countries.

London had a special appeal for Monet. In January 1900, he wrote to Alice from the Savoy: "…the sun rose…and was dazzling. The Thames was all gold. God it was beautiful, so fine that I began to work in a frenzy, following the sun and its reflections on the water."

Right: Charing Cross Bridge, Smoke in the Fog, *1902. Using pastels helped to achieve these atmospheric effects.*

THE GARDEN

Despite becoming extremely wealthy and world famous, Monet never lost the desire
to cultivate a garden that was a work of art in itself and to interpret it in his own unique
way in his paintings, at different times of day and during different seasons.

Never one to stand still, Monet had
plans to use his garden at Giverny as a
rich source of inspiration.

BACK IN GIVERNY

In London in 1900, Monet worked so
unrelentingly that he pushed himself
almost to the point of collapse. The
following year, once again in London,
an acute attack of pleurisy forced
him to return home. Still his passion
fuelled him and even while he was
convalescing, he worked on improving
his London canvases in his sky-lit studio,
and planned ways of altering his water
garden. The pond was a fair size, but
the lilies had spread and completely
filled it, obliterating any sight of the
water, so he could not see their
reflections. As this was one of his main
aims, he needed to do something.

Over the summer he discussed his
plans to increase the area of the pond
with experts. On the way he
encountered countless administrative
complications and objections and it
became a vast and expensive undertaking.

Above: Garden at Giverny, 1895. The
painting is all about the profusion and
flamboyance of the blooms. The figure is
just a small point of interest.

To build a pond so large would require
planning permission. Once this was
achieved, he had to dig ditches to
divert and bring in water from the
nearby River Ru. Local farmers who
also used the Ru were worried that
Monet would use up their water supply
and that the exotic plants in his pond
would contaminate the water. None of
the locals could understand why he
wanted to create such a huge pond in a

Left: The Artist's Garden at Giverny,
1900, provided Monet with a constant
source of inspiration.

private garden. But, it was no ordinary garden. Although gardening was a national pastime, his three acres of flowers and trees were unusual.

By the beginning of the 20th century, Monet's trees and shrubs had grown sufficiently for him to be able to paint their profusion. At that time he produced more than 30 paintings of his garden and possibly more, as it is known that he destroyed some he was not happy with, but it has not been established quite how many. However, of those that remain, approximately two-thirds of these early 20th-century garden paintings portray the water lily pond.

FLOWERS

From early on in his career, Monet painted flowers. His first revelation as he described it, came when he saw Manet's *Le Déjeuner sur l'Herbe*, which inspired him to paint his own version and also *Women in a Garden*. From then on, he rarely went for long without painting flowers, whether it was Jean and Camille in a poppy field, his father at Sainte-Adresse, his garden at Vétheuil or even a still life of chrysanthemums. The fascination for their colours and textures never left him and he once said, "I am following Nature without being able to grasp her; I perhaps owe having become a painter to flowers."

THE SPECIAL FLOWER-BED

Monet subscribed to horticultural magazines and encyclopedias, ordering seeds from around the world and consulting with friends who shared his enthusiasm for gardening. In his garden, Monet selected the location and planting of the flowers, co-ordinating their blooming periods and creating schemes for each island flower-bed. There was one exception. The flower-bed under his windows at Giverny was a copy of one that he had seen and painted at his aunt Lecadre's home in Sainte-Adresse when he was 26. As the family member who had believed in him and encouraged him to become an artist, Aunt Jeanne Lecadre had a special place in his heart and the flower-bed was a constant reminder of her.

Top: Spring at Giverny, *1903. Monet, using fairly delicate brushwork, continued his experiments, deceivingly sketchily.*

Above: Water Lily Pond: The Bridge, *c.1898. This is taken from an unusual viewpoint — not the usual close-up view.*

THE SAVOY AGAIN

Although Monet had achieved worldwide renown, his work had never sold well in Britain. He also felt somewhat disillusioned with France after the Dreyfus Affair. These factors led to him visiting London so frequently between 1899 and 1901.

Monet's interest in the English gentleman's way of life had expanded as he had grown older and wealthier.

PAINTING WEATHER EFFECTS

The most pressing reason for spending time in London, however, was to paint the thick fog that shrouded the famous buildings on the River Thames. As early as 1877 he had written to his friend Duret of his ambition to "paint some effects of mist on the Thames". More than 20 years later, the fascination remained and the effects of the pollution that hung heavily in the London air became his main focus.

From 1899 to 1901, his three visits to the Savoy Hotel in London were taken only during the winter months.

Right: The Houses of Parliament, London, with the Sun Breaking Through the Fog, *1904.*

Bad weather frequently prohibited his painting, so progress was slow, but when the weather was suitable, whether it was raining, snowing or the sun was shining, he set to work applying muted and blurred colours and contours. Every change in the weather charmed him. In 1900, he wrote to Blanche: "Every day I find London more beautiful to paint." The following year, he took with him many of the canvases that he had painted on previous visits and continued to adjust them and build up even more layers of colour to re-create the effects he wanted. He wrote to Alice, "This is not a country where one can finish anything on the spot; the effect can never be found twice." He also felt guilty that she was in Giverny, unable to recover from the depression

Left: Seagulls over the Houses of Parliament, *1904. Monet took great care to build up harmonies and contrasts.*

that enveloped her. He wrote that he was "occupied in searching for pretty colours while you suffer". On his final visit to London in December 1901 he resumed his daily routine of painting from his balcony in the mornings and early afternoons and painting the Houses of Parliament from St Thomas' Hospital in the late afternoon.

BACK TO GIVERNY

Returning to France at the end of 1901, he worked on his London canvases in his studio for three years. By 1904, he had completed 85 paintings of London, and in May of that year he exhibited 37 of them at Durand-Ruel's gallery in Paris. The sale of these works at this exhibition turned out to be his greatest success to date, with collectors from France, Britain and the U.S.A. paying increasingly high prices for them.

Later that year, his work was also included in exhibitions in Missouri, Berlin and Dublin. In January 1905, Durand-Ruel organized an Impressionist exhibition at the Grafton Galleries in London. Among the works shown, by Renoir, Sisley, Pissarro, Cézanne, Degas, Morisot, Manet and Monet, 55 were by Monet. He was included in the Venice Biennale also. Critical reviews were now a thing of the past. Monet was in demand, but rather than becoming over-confident and assured about his painting, he spent even more time deliberating over his works and trying to perfect them before allowing them to be seen by the public.

QUEEN VICTORIA'S FUNERAL

Monet was delighted to be in England so that he could spend time with English friends, and also to witness Queen Victoria's funeral procession on 2 February 1901, which he claimed was a "unique spectacle".

Above: Parliament, Reflections on the Thames, *1905. One of his series of experiments with atmospheric effects.*

Left: Houses of Parliament, Effect of Sunlight, *1903. Monet used colour with an increasing freedom in these views.*

LANDSCAPE TRADITIONS

English landscape painting had been made reputable by artists such as Crome, Girtin, Cotman, Constable and Turner, who often made a feature of its changeable weather effects. This probably added to Monet's resolve to paint in England. Perhaps he needed to paint some English views in order to prove that he was a worthy landscape painter, and to show the art world his skill.

POND OF LIGHT

At the turn of the 20th century, Monet became interested in cars and in 1901 and 1904 he bought his first and second motor vehicles. He hoped that outings would help to lift Alice's spirits and in 1904, he also took her to Madrid.

In October 1904, Monet wrote to Durand-Ruel: "I've now decided to put a long-cherished plan of mine into practice: to go to Madrid to see the Velázquez."

SELLING FEWER PAINTINGS

Monet also used his car to go on painting excursions to Vétheuil and Lavacourt. Once there, he painted familiar views over and again. But even when things appeared to be going well for him, he had doubts about his abilities. It did not seem to make a difference that his work was now well received at international exhibitions and that collectors clamoured to own a Monet – he still deliberated over and honed his work obsessively before he let anyone see it. He began making fewer sales and deliberated on his work for longer. In 1902, for instance, he exhibited just 12 paintings he had completed of Vétheuil at a gallery in Paris. Each painting was thick with several layers of paint, indicating how many times he had added, or altered, areas of each work.

By 1904, his income was such that any financial worry was eliminated. He did, however, have concerns about his work and his moods and confidence fluctuated a lot. Occasionally, enthusiasm and high spirits would take over, but more often, disillusionment and despair overcame him. Yet none of this is apparent in the works he produced at the time. Although his output was less than it had been when he was younger, the compositions he produced were as carefully considered and his application varied with each subject.

REPOSE IN REFLECTION

Once the enlargement of his pond had been completed, Monet set up his easel there and resumed painting. The

resulting canvases are calm and serene, centring on the reflections in the water. He concentrated on the surface of the water, so horizons no longer feature. Instead, the pond itself fills each canvas. Unlike the earlier Japanese bridge paintings, reflections and lilies are the only elements. Clouds and plants appear in the paintings, but only as reflections on the surface of the water and the dwindling size of the flowers alone convey the depth of the space. The human element is completely missing from any of these water garden works. In other paintings of gardens, he often included members of his family, but they are never present in his pond paintings. Another constant is that despite his self-doubts and frequently negative outlook, each water lily pond painting he executed during the first few years of the 20th century is calm and serene.

It has been suggested that Monet's disenchantment with his homeland over the Dreyfus Affair also led to his withdrawing into his garden even more on his return from London. For some time, his garden and family were enough. The Japanese bridge and the

Left: The Water Lily Pond, 1904.
Monet explored the surface of water,
incorporating flowers and reflections.

Above: Water Lilies, *1906. Monet did not consider the reflections, but focused on the tonal harmonies of the motif.*

pond supplied him with endless inspiration. He spent most of his days painting in seclusion, capturing his ultimate creation on canvas. He once said, "I have always loved sky and water, leaves and flowers. I found them in abundance in my little pool." It was a therapeutic experience and gardens had always lightened his spirits. Additionally, the Japanese influence of his house and garden was intended to be more than simply an aesthetic consideration. He was also aiming to make his home a place of sanctity and meditation. Nowhere was this tranquillity more evident than in the water garden.

These first paintings of his lily pond took six years, from 1903 to 1909. He is said to have started 150 of them and completed nearly 80.

Above: Water Lilies with Weeping Willows, *1907. This series is of the reflections of the trees around the pond.*

Above: Water Lilies (Nympheas), *1907. The water lilies are almost secondary to the shapes and rich colours on the pond.*

AUTUMN IN VENICE

At the end of September 1908, when Monet was 68, he discovered the attraction of Venice. The contrast of buildings, atmospheric light and water was too appealing to resist and perfectly suited his interests and passions.

Left: The Ducal Palace, Venice, *1908. Not understanding the climate of Venice, he used oranges and blues in this painting.*

end, he and Alice stayed in Venice for two months – twice as long as they had intended.

VIEWPOINTS
Eventually, Monet selected more than eight vantage points from which to work. The chosen locations included the Doge's Palace, San Giorgio Maggiore and the Grand Canal. Most of these offered opportunities and features that he was used to, including Gothic and medieval architecture, water reflections and elusive light. As before, only with an even brighter palette, he aimed to reinterpret the surroundings in veils of colour. He was once again captivated by a landscape filled with solid architecture, shrouded in mist and appearing to float on its reflections.

To achieve one particular view, he took a boat to the island of San Giorgio Maggiore, and also travelled to areas

By painting atmospheric views of Venice, Monet was once again following in the footsteps of Turner and Whistler.

DISCOVERY
Monet and Alice arrived in Venice by train on 1 October 1908. They travelled there at the invitation of Monet's English friend, a Mrs Mary Hunter, and planned a month-long visit. Monet's first glimpse of the city left him overcome with admiration. He is said to have exclaimed: "It is too beautiful to be painted! It is untranslatable!" Even Alice visibly brightened up while there. Initially, they stayed at the Palazzo Barbaro on the Grand Canal as guests of Mary Hunter. Two weeks later, when she was unexpectedly called away, they transferred to the Grand Hotel Britannia, farther down the Grand Canal. Monet had already decided to

work on a series there and spent the first few days researching suitable sites and visiting the churches and museums to study three great Venetian colourists: Titian, Giorgione and Veronese. In the

Right: Venice Palazzo da Mula, *1908. He finished this work in his studio, but the paint layers remain fairly thin.*

where he could see the Grand Canal and Santa Maria della Salute and the Palazzo Contarini in full view. The more he explored and sketched, the more he was gripped by the compulsion to paint there and from 9 October until they left at the beginning of December, he worked solidly. His pattern was similar to the working methods he had started at Rouen Cathedral and then the Thames series, but as he had been doing more frequently, he did not finish any of his paintings on site. He wrote of only producing trials and beginnings while there and in October, he wrote to the art dealer Gaston Bernheim: "Although I am enthusiastic about Venice, and though I've started a few canvases, I'm afraid I will only bring back beginnings that will be nothing else but souvenirs for me."

THE PASSAGE OF THE SUN
As in London, Monet's timetable in Venice was ruled by the passage of the sun. He started new canvases most

Right: San Giorgio Maggiore, Venice, *1908. When he painted this, his vision was poor and he saw pink and blue hues.*

days. From eight in the morning he set up his easel in front of the first motif, San Giorgio Maggiore, facing St Mark's Square. At ten o'clock he moved across to St Mark's Square. After lunch, he worked on the Grand Canal and later from the Palazzo Barbaro and then the Grand Hotel Britannia, painting the Palazzo da Mula. He often took Alice

Above: San Giorgio Maggiore at Dusk, *1908. This view of the island of San Giorgio was painted from St Mark's Square.*

on a gondola ride each evening. She wrote to her daughter Germaine: "The view out of our window is marvellous. You couldn't dream of anything more beautiful."

SUFFERING AND SOLACE

Although Monet's work was now productive and profitable, it was a great sadness when during the first few weeks of 1909, Alice became quite seriously ill. She died in 1911 and a few years later was followed by Monet's son, Jean, who was only 46 years old.

Although Alice took to her bed, Monet felt more positive after the Venetian trip than he had done for a while and he decided to complete some of his lily paintings in the studio.

WATER LILY EXHIBITION

After several postponements, by the end of January, Monet felt able to agree on a date for an exhibition at Durand-Ruel's gallery in rue Laffitte. In February, Durand-Ruel visited Monet at Giverny

and was sorry when he saw the Venetian canvases, since they were promised to Bernheim. Nevertheless, on 6 May, the exhibition *The Water Lilies, a Series of Water Landscapes* (the title was chosen by Monet) opened at Durand-Ruel's gallery. Forty-eight of

Monet's works, painted between 1903 and 1908 were displayed. It was five years since his last one-man exhibition and it attracted much attention. Both the public and critics were enthusiastic about the variety of effects he had captured. His work reflected his passion

THE FLOOD

In January and February of 1910, Paris and the valley of the Seine suffered severe flooding. The banks of the Seine and Epte in Giverny burst and water reached halfway up the central walkway of Monet's garden. Cut off from the outside world, with Alice still ill, it was a dreadful few weeks for Monet. His pond was completely flooded, he could barely communicate with the outside world and provisions dwindled. In February, he wrote to a friend, "We were in the midst of a great flood and I in my selfishness could only think of my garden, my poor flowers that have been soiled with mud." By mid-February, the water rose again and Monet despaired of ever being able to recover his garden's former glory.

Left: Water Lilies, *1915. Thin, broken brushwork creates the impromptu appearance of this work. The darkest areas are created with violet and indigo.*

Above: Water Lilies and Agapanthus, *1914–17. Dynamic, harmonious and with an unfinished quality, painted when his eyesight was deteriorating.*

Above: Water lilies: Morning with Weeping Willows, *1914–18, detail of central section.*

for nature and his need to use colour to express fleeting variations in a total freedom of spirit.

ALICE

Constantly depressed since Suzanne's death, Alice had been ill since their return from Venice. She was eventually diagnosed with myeloid leukaemia and was confined to bed. As her health deteriorated, Monet became distraught, and by May 1911 it was clear that the end was near. She died on 19 May 1911, with Monet at her bedside. After 30 years together, Monet was overwhelmed with grief. For months he could do nothing. "Time passes and I cannot make anything out of my sad existence," he told a friend. At the end of the year, he claimed to Blanche that he would give up painting forever. "All I can do these days is completely ruin several Venice pictures, which I will have to destroy. Sad results; I should have left them just as they were, as souvenirs of such happy days spent with my dear Alice."

VENETIAN EXHIBITION

Yet gradually Monet worked a little more on his Venetian canvases and in 1912, four years after the trip, 29 canvases were displayed at the Bernheim-Jeune gallery in Paris. In May, Paul Signac (1863–1935) who was

Above: Rose Arches at Giverny, c.1913. *Monet laid down thick impasto paint to build up the textures of the flowers.*

heavily influenced by him at the beginning of his career wrote to Monet: "I had the joy of seeing a large part of your newest works. These Venice pictures, in which everything unites as the expression of your will, in which no detail runs counter to emotion…I admire them as the highest expression of your art."

FURTHER ILL HEALTH

Meanwhile, the health of his eldest son Jean concerned Monet. Since he had married Blanche, Jean had started showing the symptoms of syphilis,

which he must have contracted earlier. Simultaneously, Monet experienced blindness in one eye. Specialists confirmed cataracts and recommended surgery – something he was determined to avoid as he could not risk losing his sight. In fear of this, he painted feverishly, producing work that was barely recognizable, with frenzied brushstrokes and unexpected colours. Early in 1914, at just 46 years old, Jean died.

FINAL YEARS

Just after Jean died, Monet's younger son Michel underwent an operation and Monet spent time with him in Paris. The sorrow of recent times took its toll and Monet retreated more into his home and garden; his travelling days were over.

The year 1914 also saw the start of the atrocities of World War I, and Monet struggled to come to terms with his depression.

LES GRANDES DÉCORATIONS

From this time, Blanche took over her mother's role in taking care of Monet and resumed her painting to encourage him to pick up his brushes. Whether from Blanche's encouragement or from his own compulsion, around the same time, the need to paint came over him as it had not done since Alice's death.

During the terrible events of 1914, he returned to the security of his garden and began painting it again, this time, on huge canvases. Despite still suffering with his eyesight, he filled them entirely with the reflective qualities of his pond. As usual, he swerved from determination to doubt, often stopping to wonder whether painting something as frivolous as water lilies was justifiable when so many were losing their lives on the battlefields. Still, he continued painting his vast water lily canvases. He painted a series of weeping willow

reflections on four canvases that measured 2m by 4.25m (6.5 x 14ft). He had not painted on this scale since his unfinished *Le Déjeuner sur l'Herbe* of 1865.

In 1915, he had a third studio built in the garden, large enough for him to paint his massive water lily canvases inside. In 1916, his old friend Clemenceau, who was now a leading political figure, encouraged him to

Above: Water Lilies at Sunset, *1915–26, borders on an abstraction.*

create further works in the same ilk. In 1917 Clemenceau was named Prime Minister of France and said he would purchase 12 of Monet's monumental

Below: Water Lilies: Two Weeping Willows, *(1914–18), left section.*

Right: Garden of Giverny, *1923. Before his eye operations, his garden featured on hundreds of canvases.*

THE WAR

In the summer of 1914, France was preparing for another conflict against the Germans. Archduke Ferdinand of Austria, heir to the Habsburg Empire, was assassinated with his wife in Sarajevo, the capital of Bosnia and Herzegovina (an Austro-Hungarian province) by a member of a group of Serbian assassins. A month later, Austria declared war on Serbia. In August, German troops began marching into Luxembourg and Belgium. After capturing Brussels, they began marching toward Paris.

canvases to honour the young men who were giving their lives for the nation. Monet continued to work on these and 60 other water lily canvases even though in 1920, Clemenceau was not re-elected. Despite this, Monet continued negotiations with the Ministry of Fine Arts and he proposed to donate the works to the nation in return for a supply of coal, which was rationed. The Ministry constructed a new building in the Tuileries Gardens to house Monet's epic works.

NEAR BLINDNESS

Preoccupied by the growing threat of blindness, Monet wrote to Durand-Ruel in the summer of 1922: "I would like to paint everything before not being able to see anything anymore." By then, he was blind in his right eye and had only 10 per cent vision in his left. With little choice, the following year, he underwent four cataract operations to restore his sight. After almost a year, he resumed work on his *Grandes Décorations*, declaring to friends, "My sight is totally restored. I am working as never before."

DECLINE

Just before his 85th birthday, Monet announced that he was waiting "for the paint to dry" before he delivered his

huge canvases to the State. However, by the following year, his health had badly deteriorated and on 5 December 1926, he died, at the age of 86, of pulmonary sclerosis. After a simple funeral, Monet was buried alongside Alice, his son Jean, his stepdaughters Suzanne and Marthe and Ernest Hoschedé.

Above: The Water Lilies – The Clouds, *1915–26, central section. These clouds show similarities to the white steam from trains at the Gare Saint-Lazare.*

In May 1927, the Orangerie in Paris, the gallery built especially for his paintings, opened to the public.

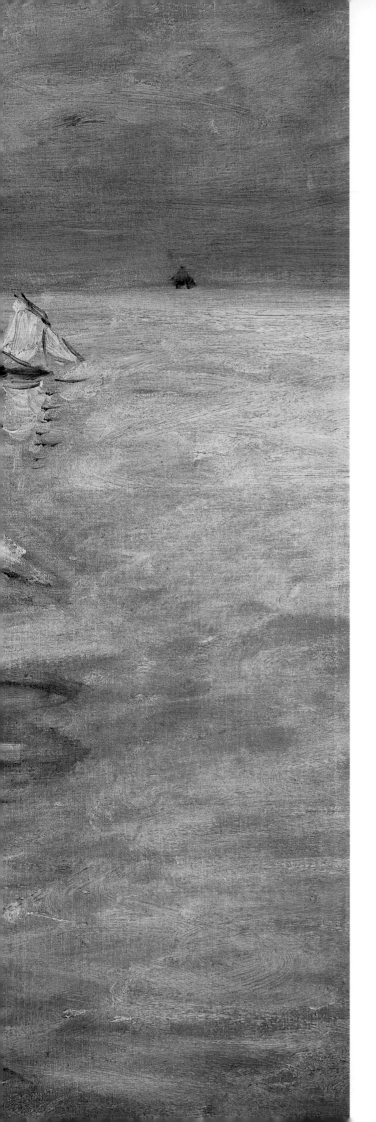

THE GALLERY

Monet saw the world as reflected by the rays of the sun, always drawing his inspiration from nature. From the moment he first painted around Le Havre with Boudin in 1858, he never stopped and by the time of his death in 1926, he had produced thousands of paintings, working on every one with a passion and intensity that never left him. Throughout his life, even through the ridicule and abuse he received in the first part of his career, he continued striving to attain something that he felt he could never quite reach. His determination never diminished and he never became conceited or complacent. In his last letter to Clemenceau, he wrote: "I was thinking of preparing my palette and brushes to resume work but relapses and further bouts of pain prevented it. I'm not giving up that hope."

Left: Small Fishing Boats at Pourville, *1882. In this simple and emotive sketch, Monet has established spatial relationships between the boats and created a diagonal composition that aids the impression of movement. Most of the canvas is devoid of action or objects, only the few boats on the water, painted in thin, smooth paint, create a focal area and the dashes add to the sense of dynamism.*

A PRECOCIOUS TALENT

Monet's natural talents were enhanced by his persistency, devotion to his art and diligence. From an early age he showed an exceptional artistic precocity, but he spent a great deal of his time doubting his abilities to capture the elusive, transitory effects he aimed for. Prolific and indefatigable, he carefully planned and prepared his seemingly ad hoc work. Starting with his sketches (he always carried pocket-sized sketchbooks wherever he went, to jot down scenes that caught his eye), he then painted directly in front of the motif and completed his canvases back in the studio, memorizing details. From the start of his career, he was always interested in conveying visual reality and in the changing effects of light on the picture he was painting. His early experimental work was a basis for what was to come later.

Above: The Tuileries Gardens, Study,
*1875. Monet caught the subtle changes
of light, from the glowing sun in the
foreground to the cool mist in
the distance. Left:* Women in the
Garden, *1866.*

La Lézarde Shores,
1856, pencil on paper,
Musée Marmottan, Paris,
France, 39 x 29cm
(15 x 11in)

Also called *House by a Pond* or *Banks of a River*, Monet drew this in August 1856, when he was 15 years old. It demonstrates his awakening interest in drawing his surroundings from direct observation. His caricatures continued to fill the pages of his sketchbooks, but more conventional drawings of trees and foliage also began appearing more regularly. This is a mature drawing for a 15 year old, with bold contrasts of dark and light tones. White pencil emphasizes highlighted areas.

Caricature of Jules Husson Champfleury, 1858, pencil and gouache on paper, Musée Marmottan, Paris, France, 32 x 24cm (12½ x 9in)

Jules François Félix Fleury-Husson (1820–89), who wrote under the name 'Champfleury', was a French art critic and novelist. In 1844, he began writing art criticism for the journal *L'Artiste*. He became a supporter of the Realist movement and edited the periodical, *Le Réalisme* in 1856 and 1857. By drawing Husson, Monet was demonstrating his early sympathies toward the more revolutionary artists of the day.

*Jules de Premaray, c.*1858, pencil on paper, Musée Marmottan, Paris, France, 24 x 16cm, (9 x 6in)

The subject of this caricature was a journalist, local to Le Havre, drawn when Monet was a teenager. He accepted that he was being irreverent, but his knack at capturing the personalities in a few confident lines earned him some pocket money. It also made him a well-known character around Le Havre.

Still Life with Bottles, 1859, oil on canvas, Private Collection, 46 x 65cm (18 x 26in)

This was one of the first paintings that Monet produced when he arrived in Paris. Inspired by paintings he had seen at the Salon and keen to show Troyon and other established artists what he could do, he painted this in a fairly reserved and academic style, keeping his brushwork smooth and paying attention to texture and tone. Even though he tried to suppress personal expression, the painting is lively and personal.

La Pointe de la Hève, 1864, oil on canvas, Private Collection, 41 x 73cm (16 x 29in)

Painted when Monet was in his early 20s, this shows the beach at Sainte-Adresse near Le Havre, which was a fashionable tourist resort at the time. It was possibly a study for a larger painting. The sketchy brushwork shows Boudin's influence, particularly the delicately rendered shingle beach and pale sea and sky. Already, there is evidence that he is interested in changing effects of light.

The Road to Chailly, Fontainebleau, 1865, oil on canvas, Musée d'Orsay, Paris, France, 43 x 59cm (17 x 23in)

With its low horizon and clear light, this shows the influence of Corot, Jongkind, Daubigny and Boudin. Monet painted this when he was with Bazille. His aims here are apparent: sharp focus of the foreground, set in lucid light with strong light and dark contrasts and small, neat brushmarks. The soft, reserved colours and shadowy trees in the background portend further atmospheric work yet to come.

Ice on the Seine at Bougival, c.1864–69, oil on canvas, Musée d'Orsay, Paris, France, 44 x 54cm (17 x 21in)

In the 19th century, Bougival was a fashionable suburb of Paris. Monet chose to paint there intermittently with Renoir or Bazille during the mid to late 1860s. His paintings capture the light and movement of the area in strong, simplified strokes. This was one of his first interpretations of a snow-covered landscape and he adhered to a fairly traditional X-shaped composition and restricted, muted palette.

Path in the Forest, 1865, oil on canvas, Private Collection, 59 x 81cm (23 x 32in)

Monet spent the summer of 1865 in Chailly. Applying earthy hues alongside some other clearer, brighter colours, this painting shows the influence of Daubigny and Corot as well as a luminosity of its own. At the time, he wrote to Amand Gautier: "I found a thousand things that captivated me here which I simply could not resist. I've worked quite hard and you will see that I looked more carefully than usual…"

Le Déjeuner sur l'Herbe, 1865, oil on canvas, Pushkin Museum, Moscow, Russia 248 x 217cm (98 x 85in)

As a tribute to Manet's work of 1863 that had shocked everyone at the Salon des Refusés two years previously, Monet produced a vast painting of the same name in the autumn of 1865 in his Paris studio after making several sketches in the open air the previous summer. He uses a completely unconventional technique of drawing the full-length figures directly on to the canvas and applying thick paint with broad, spontaneous brushstrokes.

Clearing in the Woods, 1865, Renoir, oil on canvas, The Detroit Institute of Arts, Michigan, USA, 57 x 82.5cm (22 x 32in)

During the summer of 1865, Renoir frequently painted with Monet and the other young artists in the forest of Fontainebleau. Bathed in cool light, Renoir's brushstrokes are soft and careful and Corot's influence is apparent. His handling and application of paint is vigorous and the composition is deftly constructed. Like Monet, he soon began to loosen his brushwork and to take greater risks with his painting.

Haystacks near Chailly, Sunrise, 1865, oil on canvas, San Diego Museum of Art, USA, 30 x 60cm (12 x 24in)

Painted 25 years before his Haystack series of 1890–91, these haystacks are integrated into the total landscape and do not dominate the scene. Two-thirds of the canvas is taken up with sky and low-lying clouds that lead the eye to the pale-orange rising sun.

Road by Saint-Siméon Farm in Winter, 1867, oil on canvas, Musée d'Orsay, Paris, France, 65 x 92cm (26 x 36in)

From early on in his career, Monet was attracted to Japanese snow scenes for their brilliance and luminosity. Japanese prints were printed with translucent coloured inks on light paper, so they gave the impression of a particular radiance that appealed to Monet. He painted this picture with a soft palette of white, violet, blues and brown, creating patterns out of the snowy branches that were silhouetted against the sky.

Camille with a Small Dog, 1866, oil on canvas, Buhrle Collection, Zurich, Switzerland, 73 x 54cm (29 x 21in)

On a black background, Monet – who was always keen to try out different ideas that he had seen – made a rare detour into the style of Spanish painting. Resembling work by Velázquez and Goya, this portrait of Camille is a strongly lit, carefully composed image. Predominantly red, black and white, Camille remains fairly formal and rigid, while the little dog in her arms wriggles happily – a human touch in a fairly serious image.

Regatta at Sainte-Adresse, 1867, oil on canvas, Metropolitan Museum of Art, New York, USA, 75.2 x 101.6cm (30 x 40in)

Four days after attending his son's birth in Paris, on 12 August 1867, Monet returned to Sainte-Adresse to stay with his aunt and his father, leaving Camille and their newborn son behind. The painting is of a sunny regatta, watched from the beach by several elegantly dressed spectators. With one of his favourite, low horizon compositions, the painting displays a scene Monet would have been familiar with since childhood.

Beach at Sainte-Adresse, 1867, oil on canvas, Art Institute of Chicago, Illinois, USA, 75.8 x 102.5cm (30 x 40in)

This was painted at the same time as *Regatta at Sainte-Adresse*, only the tide is now low and Monet's viewpoint has changed. Here, the focus is on the fishing boats that have been hauled on to the beach. The well-dressed figures watching the regatta have been replaced by sailors immersed in their day's work. The similarities and contrasts of the two paintings were not meant to be compared as Monet had no intention of exhibiting them together.

Seaside at Honfleur, 1864, oil on canvas, Los Angeles County Museum of Art, California, USA, 59.7 x 81.3cm (23 x 32in)

In small, rather delicate brushstrokes, this painting was executed over several sessions. As usual, Monet captured the essence of the scene *en plein air* and then completed the work back in his studio. It once again features a seascape that he knew well in a composition that he favoured – low horizon and sweeping ground, plus a ribbon of sea and some movement indicating the breeze that pushes the yachts along.

Garden of the Princess, Louvre, 1867, Allen Memorial Art Museum, Oberlin College, Ohio, USA, oil on canvas, 91 x 62cm (36 x 24in)

As with several other works from this time, there is no focal point in this scene. Instead, Monet took a high perspective and an overall view of the prospect before him as he painted from the Louvre in overcast conditions. The dome of the Pantheon rises in the distant sky and the figures are delineated with a few flicks of paint, becoming simply part of the overall landscape and not a focus.

River Scene at Bennecourt, 1868, Art Institute of Chicago, Chicago, USA, oil on canvas, 81.5 x 100.7cm (32 x 40in)

Camille sits on the riverbank of the Seine at Bennecourt. The colours of her clothes merge with the background and the light filters through the trees, touching both her and the surface of the water. Broad brushstrokes integrate Camille, the boats, buildings, water and sky while the reflections in the water create an abstract pattern. The fresh, light palette adds to the calm tranquillity of the scene.

La Porte d'Amont, Étretat,
c.1868–69, oil on canvas,
Fogg Art Museum, Harvard
University Art Museums,
USA, 79 x 98.4cm
(31 x 39in)

Dramatic, surprising and
painted with careful, short
slab-like marks, this work
explored a completely
different aspect of the
landscape that had not been
considered before. Monet
put his desire to explore
the motif before his
considerations for creating
acceptable art. Making a
feature of the overpowering
strength and scale of the cliff,
he was really exploring the
light on the contrasting
natural textures of rock, sea
and distant objects.

The Dinner, 1868–69, oil on
canvas, Buhrle Collection,
Zurich, Switzerland,
100 x 90cm (39 x 35in)

This dim interior painted
predominantly in browns
shows Monet's willingness to
experiment before he had
found his own particular
direction. Still fascinated with
the effects of light, the
highlighted area around
the table is brilliantly
illuminated, bleaching out
details and facial features. His
brushstrokes are sketchy and
give the impression of having
been applied rapidly – an
indication of his interest in
capturing a fleeting moment
in time, although he had not
yet brightened his palette.

The Luncheon, 1868, oil on canvas, Stadelsches Kunstinstitut, Frankfurt-am-Main, Germany, 232 x 151cm (91 x 59in)

Using his own family as models, this large painting is an informal lunchtime, with the vacant seat suggesting that Monet himself is about to join them. Rejected from the Salon of 1870, Monet exhibited it at the First Impressionist Exhibition in 1874. Critics were fascinated by the play of light on the table, but could not categorize the work: it was not a history, it was too large to be an illustration, it was not a still life and the viewpoint was too distant to be a portrait.

Près d'Étretat, c.1868, pastel on paper, Israel Museum, Jerusalem, Israel, 20.7 x 40.5cm (8 x 16in)

In 1868, Monet took Camille and Jean to Normandy for the first time. They rented a house in Étretat for the winter. He sketched this pastel when he was out walking. As he wrote to Bazille at the time: "I spend my time out of doors on the beach when the weather is bad or when boats go out fishing…my desire would be to remain forever in a nice corner of nature like this."

On the Boardwalk at Trouville, 1870, oil on canvas, Private Collection, 53.5 x 65cm (21 x 26in)

After Monet's marriage to Camille at the end of June 1870, they stayed in Trouville. His paintings of that time record the soft skies, cool breezes and muted light of the beach on the English Channel. Smartly attired, leisurely figures stroll out for some fresh air and the sand, surf and modern hotels of the region are rendered in muted colours.

The Beach at Trouville, 1870, oil on canvas, Wadsworth Atheneum, Connecticut, USA, 53.5 x 65cm (21 x 26in)

With its lively, atmospheric portrayal of daily life at a fashionable seaside resort, Monet changed his style at Trouville, starting to use a brighter palette and focusing on the effects of light. He had been rejected from the Salon recently, while his fellow artists, Manet, Degas, Pissarro, Renoir and Sisley had all been accepted, but this work remains optimistic, daring and confident. Grains of sand confirm that the work was at least partly painted on the beach.

Camille on the Beach, 1870, oil on canvas, Musée Marmottan, Paris, France, 30 x 15cm (12 x 6in)

Trouville was an extremely fashionable holiday resort during the Second Empire and Monet found the atmosphere conducive to his work. Judging by the work Monet produced and the images of Camille, the couple seem relaxed. This rapidly executed sketch using quick, smooth brushstrokes has captured the movement of Camille's clothes as she turns to look at her husband.

On the Beach at Trouville, 1870, oil on canvas, Musée Marmottan, Paris, France, 38 x 46cm (15 x 18in)

Even though they had little money, Camille is extremely elegantly dressed and would not have looked out of place in stylish Trouville. Here she is sitting with her cousin. This, as with all the paintings he produced there that year, is sketchily executed in thick impasto paint applied in abundant slabs of colour. Background figures are depicted in quick flicks of the brush and even Camille is simply noted down in abbreviated form.

The Seine at Bougival in The Evening, 1870, oil on canvas, Smith College Museum of Art, Northampton, Massachusetts, USA, 60 x 73.5cm (24 x 29in)

Monet painted this just before his marriage to Camille. Although money was still a problem, he was hopeful about the future and this painting shows his optimism. With the sinking sun streaking the clouds and rapid brushstrokes building up the impression of night drawing in over a beauty spot, he has captured the fleeting effects of a passing moment in relatively few marks.

Train in the Country, 1870, oil on canvas, Musée d'Orsay, Paris, France, 50 x 65cm (20 x 26in)

Uninhibited in his interpretation of the scenes before him, Monet was, by the middle of 1870, beginning to structure all his paintings through patches of sunlight and shade. Several of his works continued to be detailed, but the majority, including this, were executed rapidly and sketchily with paint applied with a richly loaded brush. He continued to introduce signs of technology and modern life into his landscapes, as seen here with the train hurtling through the countryside.

The Red Kerchief, Portrait of Madame Monet, 1873, oil on canvas, Cleveland Museum of Art, Ohio, USA, 99 x 79.8cm (39 x 31in)

Initially, this composition contained two figures seated in the room on either side of the window. Monet altered it, replacing the figures with Camille, passing outside the window in a red cape that grabs the viewer's attention. Bright light reflected from the snow-covered landscape outside floods the room, obliterating details. The loose brushwork implies a quickly captured, transient moment.

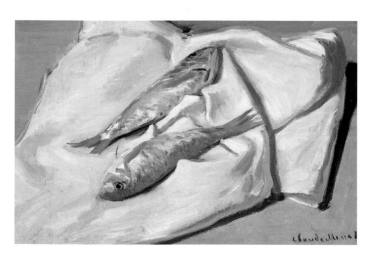

Red Mullets, c.1870, oil on canvas, Fogg Art Museum, Harvard University Art Museums, USA, 31 x 46cm (12 x 18in)

This was one of the many works that Monet painted fairly rapidly at first, and then retouched carefully over several sessions in his studio.

Although he has rendered the still life with thin, freely applied strokes, the final applications were fairly neat and precise. He intended to show how he could create an impression of solidity and realism while reducing details and enhancing the play of light.

The Jetty at Le Havre, Bad Weather, 1870, oil on canvas, Private Collection, 50 x 61cm (20 x 24in)

Monet probably painted this during the winter of 1868 when he produced over 20 seascapes, each dynamic and expressive in its own way. Here, figures are silhouetted against an expanse of wild sea and sky. The strong wind and rain are suggested in broad sweeps of thinly applied paint. A frozen moment in time is described in the leaden sky and the sodden, reflective pavements and the excitement of the huge boat being tossed on the waves is almost palpable.

Madame Monet on the Sofa, c.1871, oil on canvas, Musée d'Orsay, Paris, France, 48 x 75cm (19 x 29in)

Dark colours pull the image together, while the light from the window highlights Camille's face. Similar to Degas and Manet's interior scenes, a Japanese fan in the background alludes to Monet's admiration of Japanese art. This painting was exhibited in London at the International Exhibition in May 1871.

Boats in the Port of London, 1871, oil on canvas, National Museum and Gallery of Wales, Cardiff, UK, 48.5 x 74.5cm (19 x 29in)

As a refugee from the Franco-Prussian War, Monet painted several images of the Thames when he stayed in London for the first time from 1870 to 1871. This depicts the Pool of London with the Customs House on the right and London Bridge in the background. Both Turner's and Whistler's work seem to have influenced the colour and tone in his paintings.

The Blue House, Zaandam, 1871, oil on canvas, Private Collection, 154 x 114cm (60 x 45in)

When Daubigny and Jongkind praised Holland, Monet felt compelled to see it for himself. After he left London in June 1871, he travelled there with Camille and Jean before returning to France. The flat landscape with its canals and windmills inspired him enormously. Dutch painters of the 17th century set their horizons low, making features of the sky and Monet tried the same when he was in Holland.

View of the Voorzaan, 1871, oil on canvas, Musée Marmottan, Paris, France, 39 x 71cm (15 x 28in)

Unlike the 17th-century Dutch landscape painters, when in Holland, Monet was aiming at capturing natural impressions with relatively simple brushstrokes. Sky and water were combined in atmospheric paintings in earthy colours.

The Dam at Zaandam, Evening, 1871, oil on canvas, Private Collection, 72 x 44cm (28 x 17in)

Monet painted over 20 pictures during his five-month stay in Holland. This captures the harbour at twilight as the sky darkened over the water. Like several of the other canvases he produced there, this is painted from a low viewpoint to emphasize the sky and reflections. As in many of his works, there is no single focal point – the landscape itself is the focus.

The Windmill, Amsterdam,
1871, oil on canvas,
Museum of Fine Arts,
Houston, Texas, USA,
48.5 x 73.5cm (19 x 29in)

As well as his fascination for
the flat expanses of water
in the Dutch landscape,
Monet was also intrigued by
the windmills. This painting
shows the Rozenboom mill
on the Onbekende Canal in
Amsterdam. The mill
extracted dyes from
coloured wood that was cut
by convicts from
Amsterdam's prison. When
chemical dyes were
introduced, the mill went out
of business. It was replaced
by a theatre in 1876, but
artists continued to paint it.

The Voorzaan, 1871, oil
on canvas, Noortman,
Maastricht, Netherlands,
71 x 39cm (28 x 15in)

While he was working in
Holland, Monet was
determined to depict the
shimmering surface of
the canals with the dramatic
shapes of the buildings and
boats silhouetted against the
sky. He painted in Holland,
but worked on his canvases
later in his studio in France.
He applied brushstrokes on
top of the thinner, earlier
ones, to build up colour,
tone and texture.

The Reader or Springtime,
1872, oil on canvas, Walters
Art Museum, Baltimore,
USA, 50 x 65.5cm
(20 x 26in)

Sitting peacefully in the
dappled shade, Camille reads
quietly. Monet clearly
appreciated the juxtaposition
of his pretty young wife in
pastel coloured fashionable
attire, sitting on the grass,
surrounded by softly coloured
lilac blossoms and greenery.
All the colours are built up
with unblended dabs of
paint. This was the garden
of Maison Aubry, the Monets'
first home in Argenteuil. This
work was exhibited in the
Second Impressionist
Exhibition in 1876.

*Argenteuil, at the End
of the Afternoon*, 1872,
oil on canvas, Private
Collection, 60 x 81cm
(24 x 32in)

While Monet was living in
Argenteuil in 1872, Renoir
often visited his friend and
the two artists went on
painting expeditions around
the local countryside, setting
up their easels side by side.
Their close friendship
continued until Renoir's
death in 1919. Monet
began focusing on painting
subtle, atmospheric light,
during differing times
of day or night and
across the seasons.

The Marina at Argenteuil,
1872, oil on canvas, Musée
d'Orsay, Paris, France,
60 x 80.5cm (24 x 32in)

With delicate brushmarks
and viscous paint, Monet
built up the impression of a
blustery day, capturing the
contemporary popularity of
boating and his own love
of water and boats. In the
1870s, Argenteuil was
synonymous with boating
activities. This period marks
the zenith of Impressionism;
Manet, Renoir and Sisley all
came to Argenteuil and
painted the same landscapes.
Subsequently, they pursued
their own interests.

Pleasure Boats, Argenteuil,
1872, oil on canvas, Musée
d'Orsay, Paris, France,
49 x 65cm (19 x 26in)

Continuing on from his
experiments in Zaandam,
this also has a low
perspective, making the
water more important than
it might otherwise be. Monet
began with a soft, ochre-
coloured paint and applied
the contrasting cool greys,
whites, blues and creams in
smooth, fairly thick layers. In
marks of burnt sienna, only
the masts and reflections,
plus the small trees on
the right, introduce verticals
to the picture.

Jean Monet on his Hobby Horse, 1872, oil on canvas, Metropolitan Museum of Art, New York, USA, 60.6 x 74.3cm (24 x 29in)

This is Monet's young son in the Argenteuil garden during their first idyllic summer there in 1872. Monet did not exhibit this work but kept it throughout his life. Five-year-old Jean plays on his hobby horse, in the first garden that Monet cultivated. The paint is freely and thinly applied, with areas of bare canvas showing in places. Jean featured in several of Monet's paintings during the family's first few years in Argenteuil.

Fog Effect, 1872, oil on canvas, Private Collection, 76 x 48cm (30 x 19in)

One of the first attempts at recapturing the ways in which fog appears to dissolve solid objects, Monet painted this during the winter of 1872. He returned to the earthier palette of his earlier years. It was an experimental work in which he practised blending and dry-brushing in order to achieve the atmospheric effects and changes he was so keen to capture on his canvas.

The Robec Stream at Rouen, 1872, oil on canvas, Musée d'Orsay, Paris, France, 50 x 65cm (20 x 26in)

For this work, Monet used a softer palette than usual and he applied the paint in controlled and careful strokes. Nevertheless, in his efforts to achieve truthfulness through direct experience of nature and to capture the light conditions of a fleeting moment, he had to paint quickly. Even though this appears quite cautiously rendered, it is based on the artist's instant impressions of a view, considered, but not laboured.

Carrières-Saint-Denis, 1872, oil on canvas, Musée d'Orsay, Paris, France, 61 x 81cm (24 x 32in)

This was painted during 1872, when Monet and Camille were experiencing more comfortable financial circumstances. Unusually for this period, Monet has filled over half of the canvas with water. Normally, he put the horizon much lower down. In places, the canvas shows through the paint, indicating the speed with which he painted. Broken reflections and misty distances are themes that he returned to again and again.

Argenteuil, 1872, oil on canvas, Musée d'Orsay, Paris, France, 50 x 65cm (20 x 26in)

The Seine, dotted with boats particularly appealed to Monet. Working from his floating studio, he often painted from nature, catching the boats as they skimmed over the water at Argenteuil. This is painted in delicate, smoothly blended brushstrokes, mainly applied in horizontal marks to catch the vibrant play of light on the water. In medium consistency the paint was applied in an assured and confident manner.

Sailing Boat, 1872, oil on canvas, Private Collection, 48 x 75cm (19 x 30in)

From about 1830, boating became fashionable along the Seine and from 1850 racing boats competed at Argenteuil where the Seine widened into a basin, providing a broad stretch of water. Linked to Paris by train, Argenteuil attracted many competitors and on Sundays crowds came to stroll by the river and watch the races. From 1871 to 1878, Monet enjoyed painting the boats at Argenteuil over and over again, in different lights and weather conditions.

Red Boats, Argenteuil c.1875,
oil on canvas, Musée de
l'Orangerie, Paris, France,
55 x 65cm (22 x 26in)

Famous for its international
boating races, Argenteuil
was a perfect location for
Monet and his friends. By
1875, he had completed
many paintings of boats

there, in a variety of colours,
conditions and situations.
Here, the red boats are in
the centre of the
composition, contrasting
strikingly with the blue sky
and water and green
vegetation. The entire view is
punctuated by touches of
white, from the sails to the
reflections on the river.

The Seine at Bougival, 1872, oil on canvas, Private Collection, 95 x 48cm (37 x 19in)

With another enticing composition, Monet applied fragmented brushstrokes to this canvas, building up, in layers, the image of water and sky, punctuated by foliage and buildings. He probably painted this alongside Sisley during the warm summer of 1872.

Path through the Vines, Argenteuil, 1872, oil on canvas, Private Collection, 75 x 48cm (30 x 19in)

A dull, grey sky, a rutted path, an old wooden fence and a distant train – perhaps only Monet could turn this into a work of art. When Durand-Ruel bought the paintings Monet produced that year, he was taking a risk as they did not appeal to many people. Many of the paintings he bought from Monet at this time remained in store for several years.

Regatta at Argenteuil, c.1872, oil on canvas, Musée d'Orsay, Paris, France, 48 x 75cm (19 x 30in)

Fragmented brushmarks and bright fresh colours are built up in flat, buttery slabs to create an impression of colour, movement and warm, breezy summer air. Most of the paint is impasto and the colours are clear and occasionally mixed with white, but on the whole they are unblended. The entire image is unified through the rippling water surface and the variegated reflections on it.

The Walk (Argenteuil),
c.1875, oil on canvas,
Private Collection,
60 x 80cm (24 x 31in)

First painted in the early
summer of 1872, Monet
added to this over the next
few years, building it up,
thicker paint over thin, using
a reduced palette and some
of his favourite colours,
which included ultramarine,
cadmium yellow, cobalt,
viridian, vermilion and
cobalt violet. Available from
1859, cobalt violet was the
first opaque pure violet
pigment to appear on the
market, and Monet quickly
adopted it.

The Artist's House at
Argenteuil, 1873, oil on
canvas, Art Institute of
Chicago, Illinois, USA,
58.4 x 71cm (23 x 28in)

During his second summer
in Argenteuil, Monet painted
Jean playing with his hoop on
the terrace among the blue
and white plant pots they
brought back from Holland.
Camille, dressed in
harmonious blue, is peeping
out of the door. With short
brushstrokes, Monet built up
the textures of the leaves,
figures and flowers and the
pattern of cast shadows. This
is one of several garden
landscapes that he painted in
the summer of 1873.

Promenade near Argenteuil
1873, oil on canvas, Musée
Marmottan, Paris, France,
60 x 81cm (22 x 32in)

During his time at
Argenteuil, Monet painted
incessantly, using light colours
to achieve a unique
luminosity in this picture of a
happy moment in time.
Camille, Jean and Sisley are
walking through the flowers
and the entire scene reflects
calmness and contentment.
Over this period, several of
Monet's friends stayed with
him, in particular Renoir,
Manet and Sisley, who all
came to sample the pleasure
of painting the surrounding
fields and gardens.

*The Luncheon: Monet's
Garden at Argenteuil*, 1873,
decorative panel, Musée
d'Orsay, Paris, France,
161.7 x 202cm (64 x 80in)

This shows the informality of
Monet's life in Argenteuil
during the summer months
of 1873. With lunch over,
Camille takes their guest on
a stroll around the garden
while Jean plays with his toy
bricks in the shadow cast by
the table. This family meal
set in gracious surroundings
is very different to the
painting of the picnic of *Le
Déjeuner sur l'Herbe* of the
previous decade.

The Boulevard des Capucines, 1873, oil on canvas, Private Collection, 61 x 80cm (24 x 31in)

Monet did not want to be typecast for the first independent exhibition, so he chose work that would show his range as an artist. This was one of the five oil paintings that he exhibited, which he painted shortly before the show's opening. It was a view of the crowded boulevard where the exhibition was taking place. Resourcefully, before the exhibition, Monet had gained access to Nadar's studio and painted this glowing picture of the bustling street below.

Camille Monet on a Garden Bench, 1873, oil on canvas, Metropolitan Museum of Art, New York, USA, 60.6 x 80.3cm (24 x 32in)

Camille and a friend sit in the garden of the house at Argenteuil. For once, Monet has clearly painted Camille's features and they show her sadness; her father had just died. It has been conjectured that the note she holds in her gloved hand could be informing her of his death and the gentleman with her is thought to have been a neighbour who had called to offer his condolences and a consoling bouquet.

The Sheltered Path, 1873, oil on canvas, Private Collection, 54.1 x 65.7cm (21 x 26in)

This work was bought by Durand-Ruel in December 1873, just a few months after Monet painted it. As always, Monet deconstructed the image by focusing only on the appearance of things in front of him. Once again he integrated a human figure in the natural environment smoothly, using patches of paint that are made up of reflected, cast and local colours.

The Zuiderkerk, Amsterdam (Looking up the Groenburgwal), c.1874, oil on canvas, Philadelphia Museum of Art, Philadelphia, Pennsylvania, USA, 54.4 x 65.4cm (21 x 26in)

This was produced from sketches made in Amsterdam in 1871. Later, he made an X-shaped composition and applied loose, small brushmarks, softening the colours with white and blurred outlines, creating an impasto surface to represent the image of the place he remembered so well.

Apple Trees in Blossom, 1873, oil on canvas, Private Collection, 61 x 100cm (24 x 39in)

It is not certain when Monet first encountered the works of Japanese artists, but their lightness of touch, gentle colouring and angular compositions appeared in his works around this time. Financially, things were far from settled and he continued to struggle to support his young family. From 1872 to 1873, there was a brief recession in France and Durand-Ruel was forced to buy fewer paintings from Monet. Boudin wrote to a friend: "Monet sometimes visits; he seems happy with his life, despite the resistance his painting meets with."

Poppy Field near Argenteuil, 1873, oil on canvas, Musée d'Orsay, Paris, France, 50 x 65cm (20 x 26in)

Shown in the First Impressionist Exhibition of 1874, this was painted in the fields just outside Argenteuil. Monet exploited colour contrasts, applying dabs of red across the verdant fields and allowing viewers to catch a glimpse of Camille and Jean – both in the foreground and in the distance.

Autumn Effect at Argenteuil,
1873, oil on canvas, The
Courtauld Institute of Art,
London, UK, 56 x 75cm
(22 x 30in)

Monet probably painted this
from his studio boat and
included it in the first
independent exhibition of
1874. At the time, the
colours were shocking to
contemporary viewers, being
so much brighter than earlier
landscape paintings and
juxtaposing the
complementary colours of
orange against blue. Monet
created the autumnal foliage
and water reflections with a
small brush, tapping hundreds
of times on the canvas to
build up the stippled colours.

*The Plain of Colombes, White
Frost*, 1873, oil on canvas,
Private Collection,
55 x 73cm (22 x 29in)

Two-thirds of this painting is
a cloudless blue sky. The rest
consists of a rough plain and
some houses in the
background. The light and
shadows imply early morning
and the cold palette gives
the impression of frost. Main
colours used were lead
white, chrome yellow, cobalt
blue, red madder and French
ultramarine. Monet was
becoming particularly skilful
at creating soft atmospheric
effects through blended
colour and light brushmarks.

Mademoiselle Bonnet, 1873, oil on canvas, The Barnes Foundation, Merion, Pennsylvania, USA, 54.9 x 45.7cm (22 x 18in)

This young girl was a visitor to the Monet household during the summer of 1873. Standing quite shyly in her fashionable outfit, Monet has captured her and her pet dog, framed by greenery. His rapid, directional brushmarks and light palette catch the light filtering through the foliage, perfectly integrating the girl with her surroundings and creating a relaxed and natural appearance.

The Studio Boat, 1874, Kröller-Müller Museum, Otterlo, Netherlands, 50 x 64cm (20 x 25in)

Painting his studio boat, which he kept on the Seine near Argenteuil, Monet was studying the effects of shadow and reflection on the water. Even though it was a study, however, he took the same care over this work as he did with any of the paintings that he intended to sell.

View of Amsterdam,
1874, oil on canvas,
Private Collection,
61.5 x 100cm (24 x 39in)

Monet at this time travelled to Holland where he found the combination of buildings and water inspiring. He particularly concentrated on the play of light on the architecture. With fragmented brushstrokes, this painting is divided approximately into thirds. The buildings take up a triangular area with the sketchily rendered sky and water anchoring it all together.

The Seine at Argenteuil, 1873, oil on canvas, Musée d'Orsay, Paris, France, 50 x 61cm (20 x 24in)

The sky and water are frequently used as an excuse for the study of light reflections. Monet enjoyed including the vertical lines of the trees to punctuate the composition and structure. Applying thick paint in sweeping brushstrokes, he created a tempting composition, using the river to draw viewers into the picture. The bright golds and greens contrast with the soft blue of the sky.

THE IMPRESSIONIST

When Monet and his friends opened their first independent exhibition in 1874, they were in effect, Impressionists, as this was the first time they were given the title. Monet, always regretting that it was his work that gave the group their collective name, continued recording his sensations of light and colour in nature, developing his proficiency at incorporating the essential elements of a scene. It is little wonder he was called 'the Father of Impressionism'.

Above: Women in the Garden, *1867. The woman in the picture is modelled on Camille, who later became his wife.*
Left: The Boat at Giverny, *c.1887. This depicts the daughters of Alice Hoschedé.*

The Railway Bridge at Argenteuil, 1874, oil on canvas, Musée d'Orsay, Paris, France, 55 x 72cm (22 x 28in)

Frequently travelling by train to find suitable locations, Monet was also fascinated by them as a subject for his art. Trains were still a relatively modern method of transport, so by painting them, he was battling against convention. This painting, showing a train crossing the countryside obliquely, is captured as if in a photograph. Monet caught the textures and atmosphere using a dry brush on top of thick brushstrokes to create the delicate water, clouds and steam.

Port of Le Havre, 1874, oil on canvas, Philadelphia Museum of Art, Philadelphia, Pennsylvania, USA, 60.3 x 101.9cm (24 x 40in)

On this canvas, figures are captured with quickly painted dots and lines of colour, conveying the hustle and bustle of the busy port. Colours are bright and clear, apart from the grey steam that emits from several of the tugboats.

Snow at Argenteuil, 1874, oil on canvas, Private Collection, 54.6 x 73.7cm (21 x 29in)

As Monet matured, his interest in the changing effects of light and weather became more apparent. He applied a light-grey wash then built up thin layers and quick dabs of paint to define the objects and the figures within the picture. His decision to depict a snowfall once again reveals the influence of Japanese prints.

Railroad Bridge, Argenteuil, 1874, oil on canvas, Philadelphia Museum of Art, Philadelphia, Pennsylvania, USA, 54.3 x 73.3cm (21 x 29in)

In this version of the railway bridge, Monet broke up the heavy, overpowering architecture by the sunlight touching all surfaces. The yacht sailing by, the giant white pillars, the ripples on the river and even the steam from the train, are all dabbed with white and pale blue. Gold and amber is applied in smooth strokes, while other colours are subtly tinged with warm and cool contrasts, giving the overall image of a morning during early summer.

The Bridge at Argenteuil,
1874, oil on canvas, Louvre,
60 x 80cm (24 x 31in)

Monet created the sparkling
effects of sunlight on this
bridge by balancing light and
tone, building up a natural-
looking glow through the
application of dabs of pure
colour across the canvas.
With his usual skill he
applied both short and long
strokes to indicate ripples,
foliage, architecture, water
and sky. Rich colours and
contrasting vertical, diagonal
and horizontal lines pull
viewers' eyes around the
image of modern life.

*Sailing at Argenteuil, c.*1874,
oil on canvas, Private
Collection, 40 x 32.6cm
(16 x 13in)

From the early 1860s
until 1889, Monet painted
the Seine several times every
year. In the years that
he lived in Argenteuil, he
produced around 260
paintings, many of which
depicted the river
or its banks. Carefully
selected to capture clean
lines and the speed of a
fleeting moment, this light-
filled scene, dominated by
the white sails of the
boat, was one of the many
paintings that Monet
produced in the open
air alongside Renoir.

Corner of an Apartment at Argenteuil, 1875, oil on canvas, Musée d'Orsay, Paris, France, 81.5 x 60.5cm (32 x 24in)

Jean and Camille often appeared in Monet's paintings. This shows Jean with Camille in the background, in their house at Argenteuil. Jean stands between two of the big pots that appear in other paintings of the garden. The art critic Gustave Geffroy wrote that this scene was "above all a study of the way air and light flow into the house". Monet exhibited it at the Third Impressionist Exhibition in 1877.

Red Boats, Argenteuil, 1875, oil on canvas, Fogg Art Museum, Harvard University Art Museums, USA, 59.7 x 80.3cm (23 x 32in)

In his attempts to transcribe brief sensory impressions directly and immediately, Monet developed his style of quick, unblended brushstrokes. His palette had lightened in 1870 and the ways in which he captured sensations developed from there. He loved colour and movement and this work, with the brilliant red boat against the blue of the water and sky in tiny brushmarks, demonstrates his enthusiasm.

The Boulevard Pontoise at Argenteuil, Snow, 1875, oil on canvas, Kunstmuseum, Basel, Switzerland, 60.5 x 81.5cm (24 x 32in)

During the winter of 1874–75, Monet painted 18 views of Argenteuil in the snow. Many of them, like this one, are of a street near to where he was living. The subtle palette of grey, blue, ochre and white captures the light of an overcast winter afternoon with a weak sun struggling to break through the clouds. Careful deliberation and preparatory sketches lay behind his seemingly spontaneous technique. The subject of figures walking in the falling snow is reminiscent of Japanese prints.

Young Girls in a Bed of Dahlias, 1875, oil on canvas, Narodni Galerie, Prague, Czech Republic, 54.5 x 65.5cm (21 x 26in)

Monet, Manet and Renoir all painted Monet's garden in Argenteuil, where he had cultivated hedges, dahlias, roses, geraniums and more. The style of French gardens had become quite informal in the late 19th century and in place of precise flower-beds, Parisians adopted the freer style of English gardens. This shows Camille with a friend in the garden during a sunny summer afternoon, almost camouflaged in the flowers and cool patches of shade. All is rendered in light dabs of colour.

Camille Embroidering, 1875, oil on canvas, The Barnes Foundation, Merion, Pennsylvania, USA, 65 x 55cm (26 x 22in)

Sitting by a window, Camille is bent over her embroidery, the light shining on her work and reflecting back on her face. She is surrounded by plants in the same pots that appear in several of Monet's garden paintings around that time. Viridian and emerald green dominate the palette, with harmonies of yellow and white plus touches of vivid red to create a jewel-bright image.

Poplars near Argenteuil, c.1875, oil on canvas, Museum of Fine Arts, Boston, Massachusetts, USA, 54.6 x 65.4cm (21 x 26in)

With its sweeping composition and contrasting reds and greens, this painting captures a fleeting and ephemeral moment as the meadow is touched by a particular light. By juxtaposing discrete brushstrokes of pure colour, Monet depicted his instant sensations directly to the canvas. Here, he has captured the fresh look of light and air as a figure walks through the flower-filled meadow.

Marine View with a Sunset, 1875, oil on canvas, Philadelphia Museum of Art, Philadelphia, Pennsylvania, USA, 49.5 x 65.1cm (19 x 26in)

Framed with long grasses, this atmospheric painting epitomizes Monet's determination to capture evanescent moments in time. Orange, lavender and cobalt blue prevail on the canvas, creating an immediate sensation of a cool, breezy early morning. Clouds scud across the sky and small sailing boats glide over the water. Although the human activity is recorded by the painter, Monet's real interest seems to be the river's silver surface – liquid and light – and the effects of the weather.

*The Riverbank at Gennevilliers, c.*1875, oil on canvas, Private Collection, 61 x 80cm (24 x 31in)

Dappled, directional brushstrokes create the sensation of rapid application and spontaneity, but in fact, Monet had planned and carefully designed the entire composition. One of his skills was in changing his method to suit each subject. Initially coating the canvas with light grey, he applied sketchy marks in a loose manner, using his oil paints with the delicacy of watercolours.

The Tuileries, 1875, oil on canvas, Musée d'Orsay, Paris, France, 54 x 73cm (21 x 29in)

From the apartment of the collector Victor Chocquet, Monet painted a series of four views of the Tuileries, a public garden in Paris. Monet caught the subtle changes of light, from the grounds of the public park, to the boundaries of the city, from the glowing sun in the foreground to the cool mist in the distance.

The Coal Workers, 1875, oil on canvas, Musée d'Orsay, Paris, France, 55 x 66cm (22 x 26in)

This was Monet's first attempt at painting a sombre subject and he never painted one like it again. Workers unload barges of coal while figures and carriages move silently across the iron and stone bridge arched above them. The dark forms of the men are silhouetted against the greens and browns of the water and banks, while a network of vertical, horizontal and diagonal lines is created from the bridge, chimneys, planks, mooring cables and boats.

The Boat Studio on the Seine, 1875, oil on canvas, Private Collection, 55 x 65cm (22 x 26in)

Monet painted this sketchy canvas, resplendent in full colour, of his studio boat at a time when he had returned to themes of idyllic gardens. In his works of Argenteuil during the mid-1870s, his views of his garden or the Seine did not include the trappings of modern life that he had so frequently included in his paintings, so there are no bridges, chimneys, tugboats or trains for example, just his own little bateau atelier floating along the river.

Snow Effect Sunset, 1875, oil on canvas, Musée Marmottan, Paris, France, 53 x 64cm (21 x 25in)

Monet worked on his first landscape under snow in 1865. From then on, snow and ice became something he explored as often as he could. During the winter of 1874 to 1875, he worked around Argenteuil, which was covered in a layer of thick snow and ice for several months. Here, his whites contrast from sparkling white and soft cream where the sun catches the snow, to blue and lavender in the shadows.

Spring, 1875, oil on canvas, Johannesburg Art Gallery, Johannesburg, South Africa, 60.5 x 81cm, (24 x 32cm)

As always, Monet has chosen his angle carefully and has composed this painting with a view to drawing viewers into and around the scene. This was painted after a particularly harsh winter when Monet and many others had despaired of a thaw ever coming, so spring was particularly welcome. Creating a fusion of textures, he first applied sketchy, thin strokes and added small, more precise marks on top.

Camille Holding a Posy of Violets, c.1876–77, oil on canvas, Private Collection, 116 x 88cm (46 x 35in)

Camille sits in a reflective mood, surrounded by floral prints and holding a small bouquet. For Monet, this is quite a formal portrait, even though it remains relaxed and natural. By composing the picture out of predominantly vertical lines and capturing his wife in three-quarter length, he built this up with small, diagonal brushmarks, using contrasts of light and dark to model the soft forms and shapes.

Train in the Snow or The Locomotive, 1875, oil on canvas, Musée Marmottan, Paris, France, 59 x 78cm (23 x 31in)

During the winter of 1874 to 1875, Monet set up his easel on the platform of the station that linked Argenteuil to Paris. This painting shows the train pulling in to the station and a few passengers walking toward it. Smoke belches out of the engine and blends into the leaden sky. This work possibly gave Monet the idea to paint a busier train station a few years later – the Gare Saint-Lazare, of which he painted a series.

The Artist's Family in The Garden, c.1875, oil on canvas, Private Collection, 61 x 80cm (24 x 32in)

Vivid colour contrasts and different lengths of brushstrokes create a dappled scene. Cool shadows bathe the bank of grass with blue, mauve and green, interspersed with streaks of low-angled strokes of gold and lemon-coloured paint. The top of the canvas is dense with leaves and branches; the bottom is bright with flowers.

Still Life with a Melon, 1872, oil on canvas, Museu Calouste Gulbenkian, Lisbon, Portugal, 53 x 73cm (21 x 29in)

For his still lifes, Monet used small brushes and painted in more detail than in his landscapes. Everything is linked visually to each other here, creating a pattern of shapes and colours. The shiny plate, leaning against the wall, with its leaf pattern resembles the bumps on the pumpkin that has been cut into slices. The peaches and grapes contrast with their softer textures.

The Hunt, 1876, oil on canvas, Musée de la Chasse et de la Nature, Hôtel Guénégaud, Paris, 173 x 140cm (68 x 55in)

The natural clearing in the wood leads to the middle distance, which is also the centre of the canvas. A light glows at the end of the path, inducing viewers into and around the picture. This is an unusual subject, painted from an uncommon angle. The trees and figures are handled in more detail than many of his works, but it nevertheless still explores his chief aim: that of capturing the effects of light.

The Garden, Hollyhocks,
1876, oil on canvas, Private
Collection, 73 x 54cm
(29 x 21in)

This is another soft painting
of Camille in a summer
garden setting with a pink
path leading viewers' eyes
into and around the picture.
The elegant setting with its
hollyhocks and verdant
foliage complements the
fashionable young woman
carrying a bouquet of
flowers. With its daring
brushwork and colour, the
content leaves a certain
amount to the imagination,
while the surface marks are
extraordinarily rich.

Gare Saint-Lazare, Paris,
1877, oil on canvas, Private
Collection, 60 x 80cm
(24 x 31in)

Painted at the same time as
the other Gare Saint-Lazare
pictures, this work is slightly
different. The canvas is not
completely covered with
paint, which allows its
texture to become part of
the image. In several places,
Monet applied strokes of
paint with extremely rapid
flicks and squiggles. This
technique, added to the
diagonal composition,
gives an impression of
vitality and action.

Chrysanthemums, 1878, oil on canvas, Private Collection, 54 x 65cm (21 x 26in)

Between 1876 and 1880, Monet painted this subject several times. Interestingly, they sold more readily and for higher prices than his landscapes. Loosely arranged in a basket, the white chrysanthemums harmonize with the lightly patterned wall. Brushmarks are very precise and exceptionally neat and careful, paint is fairly thickly applied with small brushes and colours are balanced and in some places, complementary.

Lavacourt under Snow, 1878, oil on canvas, National Gallery, London, UK, 59.7 x 80.6cm (23 x 32in)

In 1878, the Monet family moved to Vétheuil, a small village on the other side of the Seine. The work was painted *en plein air* in the freezing temperatures of that winter, but completed in the studio at a later date, after the snow and ice had melted. Monet's use of pale pinks and blues accented with dark browns on parts of the buildings and trees portray the silent atmosphere of the countryside under a mantle of snow.

The Rue Saint-Denis, Celebration of June 30, 1878, oil on canvas, Musée des Beaux-Arts, Rouen, France, 74 x 52cm (29 x 20in)

Five years after painting the Boulevard des Capucines, Monet returned to the Parisian streets. This shows a national holiday celebrating that year's *Exposition Universelle*. Short, quick brushstrokes combine the vertical buildings and figures with the diagonal, fluttering flags.

Through the Trees, 1878, oil on canvas, Private Collection, 52 x 63cm (20 x 25in)

With its delicate branches and leaves, this tree became a perfect veil from which to view the river, bank and houses. Monet has given the tree a sharp focus with strong contrasts of colour and created a more blurred image through its branches. This depth-of-field effect resembles a modern photograph and was inspired by his interest in developments in photography at the time.

The Banks of the Seine or Spring through the Trees, 1878, oil on canvas, Musée Marmottan, Paris, France, 52 x 63cm (20 x 25in)

After a short visit to Paris and the birth of Michel, in 1878, Monet and his family moved to Vétheuil with Ernest Hoschedé and his family. Until Hoschedé went bankrupt, he was one of Monet's most important patrons and one of the first collectors of Impressionist works.

Michel Monet (1878–1966) as a Baby, 1878–79, oil on canvas, Musée Marmottan, Paris, France, 46 x 37cm (18 x 15in)

This portrait of Michel as a baby demonstrates a father's pride in his plump-cheeked little boy. The lively sketch might have been simply a spur of the moment execution or Monet might have planned to create a more finished portrait of his son at a later date. Whatever his intentions, the vigorous brushwork gives an impression of a moment captured in time, like a snapshot would do several decades later.

Village of Lavacourt, near to Vétheuil, 1878, oil on canvas, Private Collection, 35.5 x 73cm (14 x 29in)

Directional, irregular brushmarks, including dabs, swirls, squiggles and streaks, work together to create a dynamic and animated image. Nothing is clear; all is sketchy, most of this is scumbled and layers of paint are thin. All these factors describe a speedy execution on a breezy day by an artist who was confronted with a scene that he needed to capture instantly.

Small Branch of the Seine, 1878, oil on canvas, Private Collection, 61 x 81.3cm (24 x 32in)

Monet painted this when he was once again experiencing uncertainties in his life. Michel had recently been born and his young wife was seriously ill. Durand-Ruel and Hoschedé were not buying his work and he was forced to move. As a result, some of his work from that time seems more energetic – as if he was immersing himself in his art to forget about his problems. This painting has several thin layers in fast, descriptive marks and intense colours.

The Seine at Chatou near Argenteuil, 1878, oil on canvas, Private Collection, 59.8 x 79.8cm (23 x 31in)

Life was difficult for Monet at this time, with worries about finances, Camille's illness and his two small sons to bring up. Yet on most days, he sailed out in his studio boat and threw himself into his work even more, producing expressive paintings with forthright, free marks. The fragmented brushwork simulates the moving water, while the architectural outlines dissolve in the light.

Vétheuil in the Fog, 1879, oil on canvas, Musée Marmottan, Paris, France, 60 x 71cm (24 x 28in)

Monet offered this to the opera singer Jean-Baptiste Faure, who was already at the height of his fame and was passionate about art. But Faure refused the work, despite its modest price of 50 francs, as he considered it too pale. Monet was cross: "I was in my little boat early, waiting for the light effect. The sun came out and at the risk of displeasing you, I painted what I saw." Years later, Faure asked to buy it after all, but Monet refused to sell it to him.

The Seine at Vétheuil, 1879, oil on canvas, Musée des Beaux-Arts, Rouen, France, 80 x 60cm (31 x 24in)

With its rhythmic brushstrokes and harmonious composition, the wide expanse of water and cool colours enveloping the water and trees, an air of stillness and calm pervades this picture. Lean washes of paint and gentle dabs of contrasting tones project a peaceful image but the overhanging tree and forbidding sky contradict the appearance of serenity and reveal the artist's underlying concerns for the future.

Plum Trees in Blossom, 1879, oil on canvas, Museum of Fine Arts, Budapest, Hungary, 64.3 x 81cm (25 x 32in)

During his time at Vétheuil, which he liked because it was not yet affected by industrialization, Monet painted a number of landscapes of the countryside around the Seine. Several of the paintings produced at this time were entered for the Fourth Impressionist Exhibition, but they were not very well received.

Snowy Landscape at Twilight,
1879–80, oil on canvas,
Musée des Beaux-Arts,
Le Havre, France,
55 x 81cm (22 x 32in)

Despite freezing extremities,
Monet painted incessantly
when it snowed. Almost
oblivious to his own
discomfort, in an attempt to
capture the sensations he
was witnessing, he applied
paint in short dabs to
reproduce the luminous
effects of the snow and frost
on the landscape in the eerie
glow of twilight. The soft
blues and pinks catch the
frozen, silent moment.

Landscape, Vétheuil, 1879,
oil on canvas, Musée
d'Orsay, Paris, France, 60 x
73.5cm (24 x 29in)

Vétheuil provided Monet
with landscape views –
almost as many as Argenteuil
had in previous years. Dabs
and dashes of yellow, white,
green and blue describe wild
flowers, trees, scudding
clouds, a hamlet nestling in
the hills and an expanse of
water. The grassy bank and
the trees with their cast
shadows frame the scene.
Cool colours predominate,
suggesting a cool, early
spring day.

Vétheuil, 1879, oil on canvas, Private Collection, 65 x 92.5cm (26 x 36in)

Individual strokes of colour on a bare canvas ground create a decorative surface from which this scene of Vétheuil emerges. Pale on one side to dark on the other, it describes the sunlight falling on the landscape. When Monet painted this, Camille was seriously ill and Alice was helping to nurse her.

Riverbank at Lavacourt, 1879, oil on canvas, Fred Jones Jr. Museum of Art, University of Oklahoma, USA, 60.1 x 89.5cm (24 x 35in)

Vétheuil was a small rural village farther down the Seine to Argenteuil. Even though Paris was not far away, Vétheuil seemed untouched by industrialism and the modern age. Monet's paintings of this period consist of untrammelled countryside scenes that had remained unchanged for centuries.

Vétheuil, View from Lavacourt, 1879, oil on canvas, Musée d'Orsay, Paris, France, 60 x 81cm (24 x 32in)

It was thanks to Manet's generosity that Monet could move to Vétheuil. With the canvas showing through in places and thin paint applied in small, directional brushmarks, this seems tinged with sadness – an effect that never appeared in his Argenteuil landscapes.

The Artist's Garden at Vétheuil, 1880, oil on canvas, National Gallery of Art in Washington, D.C., USA, 150 x 120cm (59 x 47in)

Monet's family in the tall shadows are rendered in fragmented brushmarks to describe the shimmering, hot summer's day. The blue and white flower pots, recognizable from several other paintings, give the image some solidity. The entire scene is bathed in strong sunlight and the primarily vertical lines are countered by the horizontal rooftops. Brightly coloured flowers are balanced by cool complementaries in the shadows.

The Frost near Vétheuil, 1880, oil on canvas, Musée d'Orsay, Paris, France, 61 x 100cm (24 x 39in)

In 1880, Monet refused to exhibit with the other Impressionists because he had submitted work to the official Salon. This balanced and coolly coloured composition was painted in the particularly harsh winter of 1879 to 1880 when the Seine froze over. An abandoned boat is marooned in the ice, poplar trees line the horizon, while the bushes near the water sparkle with frost.

The Thaw on the Seine, near Vétheuil, 1880, oil on canvas, Musée d'Orsay, Paris, France, 60 x 100cm (24 x 39in)

When the thaw came at the end of January 1880, the ice broke in huge blocks. This inspired Monet to paint several canvases on the spot. He wrote to Dr de Bellio: "There has been a tremendous debacle here and of course I have tried to make something of it…" He painted several canvases of the spectacular break-up of the ice, each slightly different, depending on the viewpoint and time of day.

The Church at Vétheuil, 1880, oil on canvas, Southampton City Art Gallery, Hampshire, UK, 50.5 x 61cm (20 x 24in)

By 1880, Durand-Ruel was once more giving Monet financial and moral support and Alice took an increasingly significant role in his life. Once again using brighter colours, Monet built up the appearance of warm light on the greenery and church here. Strong contrasts suggest vivid summer light and short dashes of paint build up the shimmering reflections on the water.

Path through the Poppies, Île Saint-Martin, Vétheuil, 1880, oil on canvas, Metropolitan Museum of Art, New York, USA, 80 x 60cm (31 x 24in)

Monet's summer canvases from Vétheuil became lighter and more expressive than those from Argenteuil. During the summer of 1880, he painted 26 canvases. Six were painted from the Île Saint-Martin, one of the many nearby islands in the Seine. With even brighter colour and animated brushwork, his work became more subjective and personal. Interestingly, it was also at this time that he became more accepted by critics and the public.

The Seine at Vétheuil, oil on canvas, 1879–80, Musée d'Orsay, Paris, France, 43.5 x 70.5cm (17 x 28in)

Unusually, Monet has created a central focal point in this painting of a couple in a rowing boat. Using soft, feathery brushstrokes for the river and foliage and small slabs of colour for the buildings behind, this image is built up of contrasts and juxtapositions, changing what could have been a subdued image into something quite dynamic.

Sunset, 1880, oil on canvas, Private Collection, 53 x 80cm (21 x 31in)

A winter sunset scene is remarkably similar to *Impression, Sunrise*, in its sketchiness and composition. Painted in his studio from sketches, Monet prized this work highly when he had completed it and included it in the Seventh Impressionist Exhibition in 1882. He wrote to Durand-Ruel: "Above all, do not put in the big Lavacourt, which was in the Salon, but rather the big winter landscape with sunset."

View of the Seine, Lavacourt, 1880, oil on canvas, Fogg Art Museum, Harvard University Art Museums, USA, 61 x 81.2cm (24 x 32in)

One of Monet's favourite subjects during his time at Vétheuil was Lavacourt on the opposite bank. His fascination with the properties and effects of water, with its transparency, reflections and movement, continued to be exploited in many of his works, and several of his canvases, such as this one, appeared more finished than others. Shining water contrasts strongly with darker foliage, giving a gloomy feel to the image.

The Break Up of Ice, Grey Weather, 1880, oil on canvas, Museu Calouste Gulbenkian, Lisbon, Portugal, 68 x 90cm (27 x 35in)

With his attraction to winter landscapes, Monet spent hours painting out in freezing conditions. Many of these spectacular and dramatic scenes appealed to the public and allowed him to show his dexterity in terms of composition, colour and interpretation. The paintings contrast directly with his colourful summer canvases in their exploitation of his skill, adjusting his marks and palette to render the atmospheric effects of winter.

Springtime, 1880–82, oil on canvas, Musée des Beaux-Arts, Lyon, France, 60 x 81cm (24 x 32in)

The individual strokes of colour and the layers of pigment in this soft, yet bright scene are reminiscent of Renoir's approach with its multitude of marks in clustered areas. The most vigorous brushstrokes are visible on the tree and grass in the foreground. Although it gives an unfinished, just-dashed-off appearance, the canvas is actually completed, with its clearly defined forms and its compositional relationships.

Jean Monet (1867–1914) 1880, oil on canvas, Musée Marmottan, Paris, France, 46 x 37cm (18 x 15in)

This painting has been treated with strokes and lines of colour that have been built up like an old master, with green and blue worked in as underpainting in some areas. This is one of the few close-up, proper portraits of Monet's eldest son Jean. Although Jean appeared in many of Monet's works, this image provides more details about the sensitive little boy's features.

Portrait of Blanche Hoschedé as a Young Girl, c.1880, oil on canvas, Musée des Beaux-Arts, Rouen, France, 46 x 38cm (18 x 15in)

A charming portrait of Monet's future stepdaughter, this was painted during the spring of 1880 when the Monet and Hoschedé families had lived together for two years. Blanche always admired Monet and this is clearly a sensitive image of the young girl whom he later taught to paint and who cared for him in his old age. Paint has been layered on the canvas, building up all the subtle nuances of tone and colour in Blanche's skin and her clothing.

Varengeville Church, c.1882,
oil on canvas, Private
Collection,
60 x 74cm (24 x 29in)

This is one of seven works Monet painted in view of the medieval church at Varengeville; a fishing village in Normandy. The dramatic location appealed to him and he frequently mixed a golden-hued palette to focus on sunlight that emphasized the dramatic position of the church perched on the top of the cliff. A warm sunset on a clear summer evening is depicted here through the juxtaposition of light and dark tones and complementary colours.

*Springtime at Giverny, c.*1886, oil on canvas, Private Collection, 50 x 70cm (20 x 28in)

Although he did not move to Giverny until 1883, he first discovered it in around 1880. Here, his vibrant palette recreates a radiant red roof and bright green foliage of a summer afternoon. Oranges, reds and fresh greens and yellows contrast with loose strokes of cool lilacs and blues in the shadows. The agitated brushwork also enhances the impression of an afternoon in the lush, warm countryside.

Lavacourt, 1880, oil on canvas, Dallas Museum of Art, Texas, USA, 98.4 x 149.2cm (39 x 59in)

Monet painted this while still living in Vétheuil. The fairly large canvas began, like most of his works, as an *en plein air* painting and was completed in the studio. Principally a horizontal composition, he broke up the image with the central island of bushes, shrubs and trees and their reflections on the water. The predominance of horizontal lines creates a calm composition, which is underpinned by a harmonious palette of shades of green and blue.

Landscape at Vétheuil,
c.1880, oil on canvas,
Art Gallery and Museum,
Kelvingrove,
Glasgow, Scotland,
59.7 x 80cm (23 x 31in)

Monet was particularly
industrious during his
Vétheuil period, even though
things were difficult for him
personally. Experiencing
financial hardship, he often
felt disheartened about his
work, especially when critics
attacked it for its lack of
finish. Here, Vétheuil can be
seen in the background and
the large tree to the side
could perhaps subconsciously
have signified Monet's feeling
of isolation and detachment
from the rest of the world.

Late Afternoon, Vétheuil,
1880, oil on canvas, Private
Collection, 73 x 100cm
(29 x 39in)

Soft, autumnal colours
pervade this composition.
Struggling financially, Monet
was desperately trying to
encourage sales of his work
and appeal to a wider
market. No element
overpowers this image. The
softly painted distant hills
sweep around the cool
shining water; the sky
reflects on that water and
the orange and green island
works as a focus for the eye
to rest on.

Eugénie Graff (Madame Paul), 1882, oil on canvas, Fogg Art Museum, Harvard University Art Museums, USA, 65 x 54cm (26 x 21in)

Madame Graff was the wife of the proprietor of a restaurant and hotel in Pourville, where Monet stayed in the winter of 1881. When the weather was too bad to go out, he painted Paul Graff and his wife Eugénie. A humble and warm woman, she was in awe of the Parisian gentleman, but agreed to sit for him with her dog.

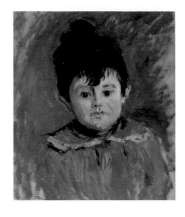

Michel Monet (1878–1966) Wearing a Bobble Hat, 1880, Musée Marmottan, Paris, France, 46 x 38cm (18 x 15in)

Monet painted this a year after Camille died, while he was still living in Vétheuil with Alice and her six children. It shows the gentle, rosy-cheeked little boy who never knew his mother, in a red jumper and bobble hat. Broken brushwork gives the impression of a lively, perhaps fidgeting toddler who had more pressing things to get on with.

Monsieur Coquerat, 1880, oil on canvas, The Barnes Foundation, Merion, Pennsylvania, USA, 52 x 40cm (20 x 16in)

With its descriptive brushmarks, this portrait has been completed with more finish than others that Monet executed at the time. Beginning with a ground made up of blue, yellow, red and white that combined to make a soft grey, he has built the skin tones, hair and features in careful layers of short brushstrokes. Far more conservative than his Madame Gaudibert of 12 years previously, this painting was almost conventional for Monet.

Germaine Hoschedé Writing, 1873, pencil on paper, Musée Marmottan, Paris, France 25.5 x 34cm (10 x 13in)

This is a sketchbook drawing of Monet's future stepdaughter, Germaine. Her father, Ernest Hoschedé asked Monet to paint portraits of his children and, in preparation, Monet produced several sketches of them at their daily activities. In the end, he did not complete the portraits as money problems overtook Hoschedé, but the sketches served as charming and informal portraits of his adopted family.

Cliffs near Fécamp, 1881, oil on canvas, Private Collection, 59 x 75cm (23 x 30in)

Simply composed, this canvas is divided up by the cliffs, sea and sky, which form curving diagonals and the sense of open space. Shifting waves and filmy clouds are set against a brilliant blue sky, creating the impression of a breezy day. Pink, ochre, blue and apricot mingle on the canvas to create a wholesome sensation of warm summer air and cool sea spray.

Poplars, 1891, oil on canvas, Private Collection, 116 x 72.5cm (46 x 29in)

The poplars towered over Monet as he worked from his floating studio. It was summertime when he painted them during a spell of idyllic weather. With the trees zigzagging off to the left, he has used intense colours and fairly strong contrasts to represent the heat of a hot summer's day. This was a location close to his home and a place he returned to time and again.

The Sea at Fécamp, 1881, oil on canvas, Private Collection, 65 x 80cm (26 x 31in)

Although each element in this painting can be determined, Monet has unified the entire scene with similar brushmarks and with an overall misty, swirling impression of wild sea, spray and rain. He painted the sea at Fécamp many times, each time in completely different weathers and depicted with totally different colours and brushwork. He was particularly adept at being able to match his marks to the style and atmosphere he was trying to create.

The Church and the Seine at Vétheuil, 1881, oil on canvas, Private Collection, 58.5 x 72.5cm (23 x 29in)

Here, the form of Vétheuil church dissolves behind the soft fronds of the bushes in front of it. The asymmetrical composition demonstrates Monet's study of Japanese prints, with the spindly foreground bushes almost blocking the subject of the work. This was nearly completed in one sitting outdoors, but he also worked on it back in his studio where he could invigorate the work with his personal vision.

The Village of Vétheuil, c.1881, oil on canvas, Musée des Beaux-Arts, Rouen, France, 14.4 x 22.6cm (6 x 9in)

Painted entirely outdoors, this is a sketch, produced as preparation for a more detailed work. This is Monet at his most spontaneous, capturing exactly what he saw before him, barely taking his eyes from his subject, but quickly dipping his brush into his paint and then swirling it on to the canvas, creating an animated image in moments.

Fishing Nets at Pourville,
1882, oil on canvas, Haags
Gemeentemuseum, The
Hague, Netherlands,
60 x 81cm (24 x 32in)

This fragile structure of
delicate poles rising out
of the sea bends in the wind,
supporting huge fishing nets.
It is an odd subject for
Monet and unlike anything
he had painted before.
Almost translucent, the
whole frame of the fishing
nets stands out against the
sea, while at the same time
it seems to be swamped
by it. Dramatic and even
ominous, the pink-tinged sky
reflects on to the nets.

*Varengeville Church, Morning
Effect*, 1882, oil on canvas,
Private Collection,
60 x 73cm (24 x 29in)

In 1882, Monet visited the
Normandy coast on several
occasions. The work he
produced there shows his
enjoyment of the colours
and textures of the
landscape there. Applying
the paint in short, curving
brushstrokes, he produced
this dramatic cliff with the
church perched high on top
of it, creating an almost
inverted panoramic view.
The colours are both
personal and representative
of the evanescent moment
he has captured.

The Cliff at Varengeville,
1882, oil on canvas, Private
Collection, 65 x 81cm
(26 x 32in)

By this time, Monet, Alice
and the children had moved
to Poissy, where Monet felt
completely uninspired. So he
spent months away, painting
around the Normandy coast.
This asymmetrical
composition juxtaposes the
calm ocean of dappled
turquoise and violet with the
bright cliffs and dramatic
dark shadows. Monet
probably worked on this
canvas over several sessions
at the same time of day,
allowing him to study the
effects of light on the view at
first hand.

Chemin de la Cavée, Pourville,
1882, oil on canvas, Private
Collection, 60 x 81cm
(24 x 32in)

The inverted triangle is a
classic composition but not
one that Monet used often,
although the path leading
away from the bottom of
the canvas toward its centre
is a favourite method of his
to lead the viewer's eyes
inward. To infuse the picture
surface with a sense of
depth, he gradually built up
layers of paint in small marks
of different coloured paint.

Fishing Boats at Pourville,
1882, oil on canvas, Private
Collection, 54.6 x 65.7cm
(21 x 26in)

In this simple and emotive
sketch, Monet has
established spatial
relationships between
the boats and created a
diagonal composition
that aids the impression
of movement. Most of
the canvas is devoid
of action or objects, only
the few boats on the water,
painted in thin, smooth
paint, create a focal area and
the dashes add to the sense
of dynamism.

The Church at Varengeville, Against the Sunlight, 1882, oil on canvas, The Barber Institute of Fine Arts, University of Birmingham, UK, 60 x 73cm (24 x 29in)

This is one of three canvases that Monet painted of the 13th-century church at Varengeville, seen from the opposite slope of the Gorge des Moutiers. Back-lit, the two trees are silhouetted against the pink and green hills, which almost seem to become a part of the church. Mist and the effects of aerial perspective soften the contours of the building and hills while the foreground foliage is streaked with gold, reflected from the sun.

Path in the Wheat Fields at Pourville, 1882, oil on canvas, Private Collection, 58.2 x 78cm (23 x 31in)

Compositionally, this is divided into three separate sections: the sky with its billowing clouds, the clear blue sea and imposingly dark cliffs enclosing it, and the richly coloured foreground with the path leading to the centre of the picture. Monet painted this carefully, using smallish, precise marks and a reduced palette of colours.

The House of the Customs Officer, Varengeville, 1882, oil on canvas, Fogg Art Museum, Harvard University Art Museums, USA, 61 x 74.9cm (24 x 29in)

This striking and asymmetrical composition owes much to Monet's study of Japanese prints. The cropped foreground, contrasting tones and colours and the lively contrast of brushstrokes help to create a complete pattern, but also the sense of isolation of the house.

Road at La Cavée, Pourville, 1882, oil on canvas, Museum of Fine Arts, Boston, USA, 60.3 x 81.6cm (24 x 32in)

The viewpoint is as if we, the viewers, were walking down the path. The path leads our eyes into the painting. the two softly curving hills on either side lead toward dark green shrubbery tipped with golden dappled reflections of sunlight. In the distance, the sea sparkles as the wind catches and tosses the waves. The same wind also blows through the long grass on the hills to either side. Describing all the textures with varied, directional brushmarks, Monet has recreated the atmosphere of a warm, breezy summer's day.

View over the Sea, 1882, oil on canvas, Nationalmuseum, Stockholm, Sweden, 64 x 82cm (25 x 32in)

During his summer visit to Pourville, Monet continued to produce dramatic cliff-top compositions. The view here is quite exhilarating and the light illuminates the hillside, creating a carpet of colours. The network of brushstrokes on the hillside is dynamic and agitated, demonstrating Monet's fresh and unique way of seeing. The contrasting colours shimmer on the canvas because of the way in which Monet applied the paint in web-like networks across the entire canvas.

*Poppies, c.*1882, oil on canvas, Private Collection, 97 x 57cm (38 x 22in)

The Art Nouveau style was emerging during the 1880s. It also developed from the interest in Japanese style, so it is debatable which style influenced Monet here. He has made the composition unique, with its curving asymmetrical lines and soft colours.

*Vase of Flowers, c.*1880, oil on canvas, Samuel Courtauld Trust, Courtauld Institute of Art, London, UK, 100.4 x 81.8cm (40 x 32in)

Using small brushes and building up the paint in layers, Monet retained the softness of the petals, while also conveying the differing textures of each object in the painting.

Rising Tide at Pourville, 1882, oil on canvas, Brooklyn Museum of Art, New York, USA, 66 x 81.3cm (26 x 32in)

Suspended high above the rocky beach at Varengeville, this house commanded a stunning view of the sea below. From Monet's vantage point, he could paint an almost bird's-eye view of the scene, incorporating the fast waves as the wind swept into the shore. He painted several views of this isolated spot, incorporating the house in its vulnerable location and always contrasting the colours, the weather effects and his application of paint, so none of them look the same.

The Customs Officer's House,
1882, oil on canvas, Private
Collection,
60 x 73cm (24 x 29in)

Monet painted this house so
often and from so many
angles that it took on a
different character each time.
Nestled into the cliff, it
seems sheltered and
compact, not vulnerable or
isolated, but simply a small
cottage on a clear, bright day.
Only the distant sea serves
to create the vast sense of
surrounding space, and the
strong contrasts of light and
dark tones capture the
bright daylight.

Cliff at Dieppe, 1882,
oil on canvas, Kunsthaus,
Zurich, Switzerland,
66 x 82cm (26 x 32in)

Once more looking down
past the cliffs to the sea
below, Monet has combined
a dramatic viewpoint with
clear contrasts. In all his
paintings of Dieppe, he was
keen to strip away anything
that was not essential. In
terms of content, these
paintings are true landscapes,
but as they were painted in
his radical manner, they
broke every convention of
traditional landscape painting.

Boats below the Cliffs at Pourville, 1882, oil on canvas, Private Collection, 60 x 81cm (24 x 32in)

Making the clear light apparent through his use of fresh colours, Monet has once again returned to ground level and has painted these boats from a direct, horizontal viewpoint. More rapidly painted than his *Regatta at Argenteuil* of nine years before, this painting nevertheless gives the same sense of airiness and yachts gliding on the water. By now though, his handling of paint was lighter and his marks more like commas than slabs.

Seashore and Cliffs of Pourville in the Morning, 1882, oil on canvas, Tokyo Fuji Art Museum, Tokyo, Japan, 59 x 71cm (23 x 28in)

Monet spent hours in direct confrontation with nature, brush and paints in hand. This was left as a sketch, without retouching in the studio, evidence of a snatched impression of the light he observed during one sitting. This painting was not meant to be exhibited, but was intended to trigger his memory of colours, lines and sensations when he painted other works.

Pourville Beach, 1882, oil on canvas, previously at National Gallery, Posen, Poland, current location unknown, 60 x 73cm (24 x 29in)

Although he never finished this, it is a good example of how Monet laid down his first, expressive marks. Using calligraphic brushstrokes and an almost scribbled technique, he created an immediate impact with a sweeping composition. In February 1882, he returned to Pourville alone and during the summer months stayed there with Alice and the children. This was painted in the summer.

The Chef (Monsieur Paul), 1882, oil on canvas, Österreichische Galerie, Vienna, Austria, 64 x 51cm (25 x 20in)

Also known as Père Paul, this man ran a hotel and restaurant in Pourville called *À la Renommée des Galettes* with his wife Eugénie. Madame and Monsieur Paul welcomed Monet during his stay in Pourville that February. As it was out of season, they made a great fuss of him, frequently offering him Paul's speciality of galettes – delicious round, flat crusty cakes.

Chrysanthemums, 1882, oil on canvas, Metropolitan Museum of Art, New York, USA, 100.3 x 81.9cm (39 x 32in)

Usually turning to still lifes or portraits when the weather was too bad, Monet frequently painted garden flowers and several versions of chrysanthemums were produced from 1877 to 1883. With their careful and detailed brushwork, the attention to detail and their strong sense of modelling through dark and light tones, these were all desired by collectors as they were very saleable. Monet sold this painting to Durand-Ruel soon after he had finished it.

Cliff Walk at Pourville, 1882, oil on canvas, Art Institute of Chicago, Illinois, USA, 66.5 x 82.3cm (26 x 32in)

From February to April 1882, Monet stayed in the little fishing village of Pourville. The young women strolling on the cliff are probably Marthe and Blanche, the eldest Hoschedé daughters. He has captured the blustery summer breeze and the sparkle of sunlight on the sea.

Boats on the Beach at Étretat,
1883, oil on canvas, Musée
d'Orsay, Paris, France,
66 x 81cm (26 x 32in)

Étretat was a fashionable
resort, which was why
Monet chose to go out of
season. The place still
appealed to him as it had
done in 1870. He wrote to
Alice: "…you cannot imagine
how beautiful the sea has
been these last two days. But
what talent would be
needed to show it, it would
drive you mad." Even
Maupassant (1850–93)
enthused about the crescent
shaped beach, which Monet
has painted here, along with
the wild sea and colourful
fishing boats.

Ice Melting near Vétheuil,
1880, oil on canvas, Private
Collection, 65 x 91.5cm
(26 x 36in)

Originally painted in 1880,
Monet completed this in his
studio three years later.
Unlike the earlier paintings of
the thaw when he was
suffering personally, this
shows his happier, more
settled state. The colours are
intense and the handling of
the paint is smooth. The
glassy reflections in the water
contrast with the freezing
foggy air. Blues and greens
enhance the sense of
bitter cold.

The Valley of la Falaise, Calvados, France, 1885, oil on canvas, Private Collection, 73 x 92cm (29 x 36in)

In autumnal colours, with vigorous brushmarks, this painting is unusual for Monet in that the tree is approximately in the centre and there are relatively few details in the foreground. Any slight details are centralized in the middle ground to lead viewers' eyes toward the house. This is also enhanced by the green band of grass that shines out amid the blends of browns, rusts and pinks.

The Seine at Port-Villez, 1883, oil on canvas, Private Collection, 60.5 x 100.5cm (24 x 40in)

Particularly relishing portraying the seasons and their effects, this image of summer turning to autumn was irresistible to Monet. Textural, colourful vegetation turns from intense green to warm gold and reflects on to the still, glass-like river in the bottom half of the canvas.

White Poppy, 1883, oil on canvas, Private Collection, 128.5 x 37cm (51 x 15in)

Emphasizing the elongation of this slender flower and clearly enjoying painting its sinuous lines, Monet has kept his palette to a minimum with blue-green leaves, soft white petals and a flower-patterned vase. He included violet in the shadows of the leaves as a complement to the yellow background. On a long, thin canvas, he purposefully exploited the influence of the Japanese style he admired so much.

Marguerites Jaunes (Yellow Daisies), 1883–84, oil on canvas, Private Collection, 15.3 x 39.5cm (6 x 16in)

This was a sketch that Monet produced as a design for a door panel in Durand-Ruel's drawing room at 35 rue de Rome, Paris. Durand-Ruel commissioned him to decorate the four sets of double doors in his Parisian apartment and Monet spent from 1882 to 1885 working on them. The final panels consisted of bright flowers and fruit, glowing out boldly and cheerfully in a fairly dark room.

Michel Monet (1878–1966) in a Blue Jumper, 1883, oil on canvas, Musée Marmottan, Paris, France, 46 x 38cm (18 x 15in)

Rather like snapshots to record his children as they grew up, Monet painted a few quick portraits in natural and relaxed poses every now and then. Rendered with divergent brushmarks, it is obvious that Michel is at ease with the artist's scrutiny (and the smell of his oil paints) as he sits, patiently, waiting for his father to finish.

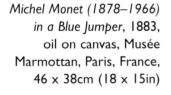

Morning at Étretat, 1883, oil on canvas, Private Collection, 63 x 81cm (25 x 32in)

Always fascinated by seascapes, Monet was enthralled by the grandeur of the massive cleft cliff at Étretat and he loved the expanse of sea around the coast there. He wrote to Alice, "there is nothing like these cliffs anywhere". Although it was not his aim as a rule, he emphasized the isolated aspect of the beaches and cliffs by painting them receding against the rough sea and sky.

Étretat, Sunset, 1883, oil on canvas, Private Collection, 60 x 80.5cm (24 x 32in)

Monet rendered fleeting effects of light and weather on the scenes he painted. By the early 1880s, he was working simultaneously on several canvases so he could depict the same subject at different times of day. He painted this view, over and again. As the setting sun sinks, it tinges the sea and sky with a fiery pink.

By the River at Vernon, 1883, oil on canvas, Private Collection, 65 x 81cm (26 x 32in)

This scene is bathed in the early afternoon sunlight, with short shadows and colourful reflections. Monet's brushstrokes are bold and confident and the surface of the painting is broken up with small marks, some in thick, impasto paint, other areas in thinner paint. Fresh and vivid colours feature, with pinks, blues, yellows, greens, purples and whites delineating the buildings and trees on the river.

Little Islands at Port-Villez, 1883, oil on canvas, Private Collection, 65.6 x 93cm (26 x 37in)

In the summer of April 1883, he set up his easel opposite Port-Villez and began painting rapidly, racing against time and its inevitable changes to the light and atmosphere. Monet's natural ability to create decorative effects is evident in his rhythmic brushstrokes.

Rough Sea at Étretat, 1883, oil on canvas, Musée des Beaux-Arts, Lyon, France, 81 x 100cm (32 x 39in)

The sun had shone during the early part of Monet's stay in Étretat, but after several days, became stormy. Forced to abandon a particularly large painting, he first frantically tried to capture what he saw, but soon lost confidence and decided that his work was inadequate. This was a difficult image to capture in view of the weather, but he had a distant, slightly sheltered vantage point that enabled him to encompass a vast expanse of the cliffs, beach, water and sky.

Self-Portrait in his Atelier,
*c.*1884, oil on canvas,
Musée Marmottan, Paris,
France, 85 x 54cm,
(33 x 21in)

Only three self-portraits
are known to have been
painted by Monet. Here,
wearing a beret and sitting
in his studio with the

inevitable cigarette
suspended from his lips, he
appears to be contemplating
a painting before he jumps
up to add something to it.

This is a good example of
one of his methods of
working, with the first layers
of paint applied in thin,
expressive marks.

The Red Road, 1884, oil on canvas, Private Collection, 65 x 81cm (26 x 32in)

On 2 February 1884, Monet wrote to Theodore Duret from the Mediterranean: "This is fairytale country. I do not know where to look first. It is all extraordinarily beautiful and I want to paint everything." In response, he brightened his palette considerably, boldly including fresh pigments he had not tried before, such as turquoise, pink and a soft shade of orange.

View of Ventimiglia, 1884, oil on canvas, Art Gallery and Museum, Kelvingrove, Glasgow, Scotland, 65 x 91.7cm (26 x 36in)

When Renoir and Monet visited the Mediterranean in December 1883, Renoir said it allowed them to use beautiful colours. Even though it was only April, the heat haze that pervades the air creates a soft blue bloom to everything it touches. Monet loved this part of Italy and worked furiously on several canvases before he left to return to France.

Monte Carlo: View of Roquebrune, 1884, oil on canvas, Private Collection, 64.7 x 80cm (25 x 31in)

In the South of France, he painted several canvases speedily and sketchily. Here, even though the colours are predominantly purples, there are greenish shades in the foliage that frames the canvas and a glow of white that implies distant hills.

Cap Martin, 1884, oil on canvas, Musée des Beaux-Arts, Tournai, Belgium, 65 x 81cm (26 x 32in)

A dramatically dark pile of rocks contrast with the cool turquoise of the sea, where in the distance, the water's surface is broken by a small yacht being tossed on the waves. Directional brushstrokes describe the trees that grow wildly, bending toward the coast and swirling, energetic marks pick out the white foam as the waves crash against the rocks.

Sasso Valley Sun Effect, 1884, oil on canvas, Musée Marmottan, Paris, France, 65 x 81cm (26 x 32in)

This valley captivated Monet with the enthusiasm he felt for the entire area. Close to the Nervia valley, it was as picturesque as other parts of the Mediterranean and he wanted to spend more time painting it. In letters to Alice, he described features of a square villa hidden under exotic foliage. The canvases he produced were executed with vigorous brushstrokes and filled with colour.

Haystack at Giverny, 1884–89, oil on canvas, The Pushkin Museum of Fine Arts, Moscow, Russia, 51 x 63cm (20 x 25in)

For several years, Monet included haystacks in his paintings of the Giverny countryside. Their role was transient and simply part of the landscape, the changing weather and light.

The Castle of Dolceacqua, 1884, oil on canvas, Musée Marmottan, Paris, France, 92 × 73cm (36 × 29in)

Monet sent Alice photographs of this area, describing it in a letter: "…two photographs of the area I went to see yesterday, Dolce Acqua, in the Nervia valley. They're not well taken and only give an imperfect idea of the place, which is superb…there's a bridge that is a treasure of lightness." The bridge rose over a torrential river, linking Dolceacqua castle with the neighbouring village.

Basket of Grapes, Quinces and Pears, 1883, oil on canvas, Private Collection, 51.2 x 38cm (20 x 15in)

One of Monet's major tasks during the years of 1882 to 1885 was to decorate the panels on Durand-Ruel's apartment doors. In all, he produced 36 paintings for the door panels of which this was one. They all consisted of fruit or flowers and all were painted in fresh, bright colours, arranged in unusual groupings and all with a luscious, shiny bloom.

Palm Tree at Bordighera, c.1884, oil on canvas, Private Collection, 61.3 x 74cm (24 x 29in)

When Monet travelled south to Bordighera in the early weeks of 1884, he was keen to explore the exuberant vegetation and clear light once more. He wrote to Alice: "The palms will make me despair....So much blue in the sea and the sky it is impossible!" Here, he has painted the vibrantly coloured plants that grow abundantly there, with the snow-covered mountains in the background.

Portrait of an English Painter, Bordighera, 1884, oil on canvas, Tel Aviv Museum of Art, Israel, 52 x 41cm (20 x 16in)

During his visit to Bordighera, Monet painted five pictures a day. As it was January and February, the weather was not as settled as it would have been had he visited in the summer. Some days were hot, while others were cold and windy. He developed headaches, a raised temperature and a cold, so he stayed in for a couple of days and painted this portrait of an English artist he met while staying at the Pension Anglaise.

The River Epte at Giverny, 1884, oil on canvas, Private Collection, 72.9 x 92cm (29 x 36in)

In the spring of 1883, Monet decided to find a permanent home for his family and he chose the small and pretty village of Giverny, which seemed to have avoided industry and the trappings of modern life. Hills, wheat and poppy fields and flower-filled meadows surrounded the village. The River Epte, a tributary of the Seine, ran near to the house he chose on the outskirts of the village.

Cliffs at Étretat after the Storm by Gustave Courbet, 1870, oil on canvas, Musée d'Orsay, Paris, France, 133 x 162cm (52 x 64in)

Monet's visits to Étretat during the 1880s possibly derived from earlier visits by Delacroix and Courbet. He owned a Delacroix watercolour of Étretat and in 1882, a Courbet retrospective exhibition included a group of Étretat seascapes. He said: "I reckon on doing a big canvas on the cliff of Étretat, although it's terribly audacious of me to do that after Courbet who did it so well, but I'll try to do it differently."

Poppy Field in a Hollow near Giverny, 1885, oil on canvas, Boston Museum of Fine Arts, Boston, Massachusetts, USA, 65 x 81cm (26 x 32in)

In 1883 Monet had signed a long-term lease for the house in Giverny. The fields of poppies and wheat near the house became a favourite subject for him before his garden was fully developed. The poppies offered a luxuriant splash of complementary colours. Although he travelled during the early years of their life at Giverny, in 1884, he had written to Alice: "If I am happy to work in this beautiful area, my heart is always at Giverny."

The Sailing Boat, Evening Effect, 1885, oil on canvas, Musée Marmottan, Paris, France, 54 x 65cm (21 x 26in)

In autumn 1885, Monet returned to Étretat, staying in the house of the singer and collector Faure. Resuming his painting of the cliffs, he began focusing even more on the fishing boats on the sea and beach. He also spent time with Maupassant who wrote of him: "…face to face with his subject he would sit and wait, watching the sky and shadows, gathering up a falling ray or passing cloud in several dabs of the brush and setting it down on his canvas with great alacrity."

The Road to Giverny, Winter, 1885, oil on canvas, Private Collection, 48 x 59.8cm (19 x 23in)

Returning to a popular composition of a sweeping path leading viewers into the picture, Monet painted this near to his house in Giverny. As well as composition, he also returned to his technique of setting up his easel in the bitter cold and painting the snow. Most of this dazzlingly lit scene was painted en *plein air*, but he completed it later in his studio.

Haystacks, 1885, oil on canvas, Private Collection, 65 x 81cm (26 x 32in)

This image predates Monet's series paintings of the haystacks but was painted in the same geographical area. The work, built up with directional, frequently diagonal brushmarks in his usual brightly coloured, but fairly reduced palette, depicts the dappled sunlight on the haystacks, shielding the two figures who sit there. The haystack throws cool shadows across the field, offering respite from the hot summer sun.

Spring, River Bank at Epte, 1885, oil on canvas, Private Collection, 64.7 x 81.3cm (25 x 32in)

Monet was charmed by the scenery around Giverny as much as he had been years earlier by Argenteuil and Vétheuil. In the spring of 1885, he spent most days in the vicinity, painting the picturesque sights around him. This suited both Monet and Alice – Monet was close to his family and his studio, and Alice could keep an eye on Monet.

The Seine at Port-Villez in Winter, 1885, oil on canvas, Private Collection, 73 x 93cm (29 x 37in)

During the summer of 1885, Monet took Alice and the children on another holiday to Étretat, staying in Faure's house, which he kindly lent to them. At the beginning of October, Alice returned to Giverny, taking the children with her but leaving Monet behind. The cold and rain did not stop him from working outside and he started hundreds of canvases.

The Rock Needle and the Porte d'Aval, c.1885, oil on canvas, Fitzwilliam Museum, University of Cambridge, UK, 65 x 81cm (26 x 32in)

Maupassant visited Monet during his stay once again and described the rigorousness with which he painted: "He took [his canvases] up or abandoned them as the changing sky changed. I once saw him catch a sparkling shaft of light on a white cliff and fix it to a rush of yellows that gave an eerily precise rendering of the blinding ineffable effect of its radiance."

Winter at Giverny, 1885, oil on canvas, Private Collection, 64.5 x 88.5cm (25 x 35in)

Rendering the mist and fog that permeated the winter air, Monet created a monochrome image through mixing pigments to create tertiary colours. This is one of Monet's unusual compositions, with the houses appearing in the foreground and also in the background. The high viewpoint and the sweeping, snow-covered hill with agricultural ruts prevent the picture from feeling enclosed.

Cliffs and the Porte d'Amont, Morning Effect, 1885, oil on canvas, Musée Marmottan, Paris, France, 50 x 61cm (20 x 24in)

Monet's compulsion to paint meant that he often left Alice and the children for weeks or even months. At each location he got up early and began painting earnestly until nightfall. It was not merely a case of self-discipline, but an inner necessity. Maupassant later remembered long walks with him, searching for suitable sites to paint and he described several of the places in his novels.

The Cliff at Étretat, c.1885, pastel on grey paper, Musée Marmottan, Paris, France, 21 x 37cm (8 x 15in)

Monet often used pastels as preliminary sketches, relishing their rich colours and immediate effects. This rapidly executed work in simple slabs of colour demonstrates his control of the medium. He wrote to Alice in October 1885: "Étretat is becoming more and more amazing…I rage at my inability to express it all better. You would need to use both hands and cover hundreds of canvases."

Branch of the Seine at Giverny, 1885, oil on canvas, Musée Marmottan, Paris, France, 65 x 92cm (26 x 36in)

Although Monet was rapidly becoming free of money worries, by the age of 45 he was still making appeals to Durand-Ruel. Despite financial concerns, he continued painting persistently and entertaining his friends when they visited him at Giverny. This vigorous work is painted with lively, descriptive brushstrokes and a palette that predominantly features blue, green and violet.

The Cliff of Aval, Étretat,
1885, oil on canvas, Israel
Museum, Jerusalem, Israel,
65 x 92cm (26 x 36in)

As well as painting, Monet
wrote many letters to Alice
when he was away from her.
One letter described how a
large wave had unexpectedly
thrown him against the cliff
and had sucked away his
easel and canvas. The next
day, he sat away from the
sea at the top of a cliff and
painted this, even though it
was extremely windy.

The Poppy Field near Giverny,
1885, oil on canvas, Musée
des Beaux-Arts, Rouen,
France, 66 x 81.5cm
(26 x 32in)

The theme of poppies had
long appealed to Monet with
its naturally bright colours
and contrasts. These poppies
are like a carpet and the sky
seems almost like a canopy
or ceiling. The image is
divided approximately
into thirds, which is
subconsciously appealing to
the viewer. Each third is
painted in a different way;
the bottom blanket of
poppies is painted with
delicate, small marks; the
distant hills, trees and houses
are painted with small
swirling marks; and the sky is
rendered in longer, looser,
diagonal strokes.

Rocks at Port Coton, the Lion Rock, 1886, oil on canvas, Fitzwilliam Museum, University of Cambridge, UK, 65 x 81cm (26 x 32in)

Painted during Monet's first visit to the west coast of Brittany in the autumn and winter of 1886, this is one of the 39 paintings he produced there. Intending to stay for only ten days, he ended up remaining for ten weeks, entranced by the wild sea, which made the waves at Étretat seem calm. Monet was particularly sensitive to the different 'moods' of water.

Portrait of Poly, Fisherman at Belle Île, 1886, oil on canvas, Musée Marmottan, Paris, France, 74 x 53cm (29 x 21in)

In September 1886, Monet went to stay with the journalist, novelist and playwright Octave Mirbeau, in Nourmoutier. There he met a character of the area, Hippolyte Guillaume. Nicknamed 'Poly' and known for his variety of jobs, he took on the roles of porter and model for Monet for two francs a day. Monet wrote: "I got old man Poly to pose and I made a good quick sketch of him, a very good likeness; the whole village had to see it."

Woman with Parasol turned to the Left, 1886, oil on canvas, Musée d'Orsay, Paris, France, 131 x 88cm (52 x 35in)

Alice's third daughter Suzanne inspired Monet to paint two versions of this picture. Suzanne was 18 at the time and possibly reminded him of Camille, whom he had painted in a similar pose several years before. He painted her against the light, barely sketching her features, but capturing instead the play of light and shade created by the sunshade.

Fishing Boats Leaving Étretat, 1886, oil on canvas, Pushkin Museum of Fine Arts, Moscow, Russia, 60.8 x 81cm (24 x 32in)

Taking a high viewpoint, with the light coming from the upper left corner of the canvas, a rosy glow is diffused on to the image.

The cliff face and shadow on the water have cool violet tones that accentuate the carved-out edge of the cliff. The area had become a popular holiday resort for Parisians, which may have given Monet more incentive to paint there and to reach a growing market.

The Manneporte near Étretat, 1886, oil on canvas, Metropolitan Museum of Art, New York, USA, 81.3 x 65.4cm (32 x 26in)

Monet could not be persuaded to take part in the eighth and last Impressionist exhibition in 1886 because of differences between him and some of his fellow artists. He does not seem to have missed it and spent a lot of time painting in Étretat. He painted this vast and dramatic cliff over six times; another early example of his method of painting in series which was to follow.

Tulip Fields near Leiden, 1886, oil on canvas, Gemeentemuseum, The Hague, Netherlands, 59.7 x 73.2cm (23 x 29in)

In April 1886, Monet was invited to Holland by the Secretary of the French Embassy in The Hague. Delighting in the tulip fields, he also added a brief clue about where he was with the windmill and flat canal.

L'Aiguille and the Porte d'Aval, Étretat, 1886, oil on canvas, Private Collection, 73.5 x 92.3cm (29 x 36in)

Monet has applied short, diagonal brushstrokes to build up the waves and to create the ground and rocks. Despite the wind that threatened to dash his canvas, paints and easel to the sea far below, he captured enough of what he needed to complete this back in the studio.

The Manneporte, 1885, oil on canvas, Philadelphia Museum of Art, Philadelphia, Pennsylvania, USA, 65.4 x 81.3cm (25 x 32in)

At the end of January 1883, Monet went to stay at Étretat. His hotel was on the beach, looking out to sea and he was delighted with it. He said, "My subjects are at the door of the hotel and there is even a superb one from my window."

Springtime, 1886, oil on canvas, Fitzwilliam Museum, University of Cambridge, UK, 64.8 x 80.6cm (25 x 32in)

This is the orchard at Giverny. Jean and Suzanne sit under the trees in the dappled light. The concentration of colour in deliberate bands painted in directional marks draws viewers' eyes toward the two figures. Monet painted the lighter, white blossoms at the top of the canvas, keeping the focus on the bottom and middle of the work.

Port Domois at Belle Île, 1886, oil on canvas, Galerie Daniel Malingue, Paris, France, 65 x 81cm (26 x 32in)

Monet was undeterred by the prevailing weather conditions; he painted at Belle Île in the wind and rain, working furiously against the elements. He used contrasts of warm and cool colours and different lengths of brushstroke to create a rhythmic, almost patterned composition. Monet built up the canvas with layers of paint that are predominantly cobalt blue and burnt sienna; the effect gives the impression that the cliffs are textured and shadowed. Short broken marks of lighter colours create the dramatic, swirling motion of the sea.

Floods at Giverny, 1886, oil on canvas, Private Collection, 65 x 81cm (26 x 32in)

In late 1886, Monet spent most of his time at Giverny, painting. It was a wet season and he responded to the gloomy flood waters under the overcast sky. Using small, almost comma-like brushmarks in a similar style to Pissarro and Sisley, these works are sensitive and capture the dismal nature of the weather at the time.

Storm off the Coast of Belle Île, 1886, oil on canvas, Musée d'Orsay, Paris, France, 65 x 81.5cm (26 x 32in)

As he tended to do everywhere that inspired him, Monet sat out in all weathers at Belle Île, capturing the motif before him, despite battering winds and pounding rain. Facing what was known as the wild west coast of the island, he wrote to Alice: "…it is superb, but so different from the Channel that I will need time to get used to it; the sea is magnificent and the rocks are a mass of grottoes, spikes and extraordinary needles."

The Boat, 1887, oil on canvas, Musée Marmottan, Paris, France, 146 x 133cm (57 x 52in)

Monet constantly looked at the world as potential canvases. This dramatic composition with the boat tucked into the top right corner draws viewers' eyes around the work. It is not clear what is river and what is vegetation, since grasses and a cluster of leaves add emerald shades to the deep blues and violets of the water.

White Clematis, 1887, oil on canvas, Musée Marmottan, Paris, France, 92 x 52cm (36 x 20in)

After a two-week visit to London with his friend Whistler, Monet spent most of the summer of 1887 in his garden and around Giverny. He painted several figures in the landscape and flowers. Sometimes, as here, he painted flowers without a landscape around them. By this time, he had many admirers within the art world and this painting was received well by many of the guests he welcomed to his home that year.

Poppy Field, 1890,
oil on canvas, Hermitage,
St Petersburg, Russia,
60.5 x 92cm (24 x 36in)

Attracted by the blanket of bright red poppies that waved in the breeze, Monet focused on their colour and movement in the wind. Details were not important to him here; he was more interested in creating a pattern with the paint marks and colours. Once again he divided the composition into three bands: the flowers, the trees and hills in the background, and the sky.

Port-Goulphar, Belle Île, 1887,
oil on canvas, Art Gallery
of New South Wales,
Sydney, Australia,
81 x 65cm (32 x 26in)

The paint is fairly thick in places, layered heavily to emphasize the rough features within the picture. The horizon of this image is concealed by the rocks of Belle Île, which rise doggedly from the sea. Almost enclosed by the promontories, the rough sea fits into an almost upside-down triangular shape although there is a small opening at the top right-hand corner.

The Small Haystacks, 1887, oil on canvas, Private Collection 65 x 100cm (26 x 39in)

Painted in the gathering dusk, these small haystacks caught Monet's eye when he was working around Giverny during the late summer of 1887. This was the start of his fascination with haystacks. He had painted them before, but at this point, he decided to look further into the textures and colours of the hay under different light effects. He produced several canvases featuring haystacks before he began his series of them.

Meadow at Giverny, 1888, oil on canvas, Hermitage, St Petersburg, Russia, 92.5 x 81.5cm (36 x 32in)

The meadows and fields around Giverny appealed to Monet as places where he could capture the fresh look of light and air. The area was relatively untouched by industrialism and as such, in his paintings of Giverny and the surrounding area, he rarely included any of the symbols of it, such as trains, bridges or buildings, as he had done in previous villages he had lived in.

Antibes, View of the Cap, Mistral Wind, 1888, oil on canvas, Private Collection, 65 x 81.2cm (26 x 32in)

To contrast with his paintings of Brittany and Normandy, in 1888, Monet returned to the Riviera. He intended to fill his canvases with soft, warm colours, such as azure and yellow and not to be battered by the elements as he tried to paint. He wrote: "After terrible Belle Île, this is going to be tender, here there's nothing but blue, rose and gold."

Antibes: Morning, 1888, oil on canvas, Philadelphia Museum of Art, Philadelphia, Pennsylvania, USA, 65.7 x 82.1cm (26 x 32in)

Monet's Antibes paintings of 1888 have a similar look and mood to the paintings he produced in Bordighera in 1884, but his colours have more unity; they are not simply a blaze of colour, but blend through greens, blues and golds, with touches of pink and orange. This was one of the works that Monet included in his joint exhibition with Rodin.

Bend in the Epte River near Giverny, 1888, oil on canvas, Philadelphia Museum of Art, Philadelphia, Pennsylvania, USA, 73.7 x 92.9cm (29 x 37in)

Applying small flicking brushmarks and variegated colours, Monet created the appearance of the sun glittering on the trees and filtering through to the river. Creating form through colour, his light and subtle approach captures the effects of clear, midday sunlight on a still, peaceful day. This was executed with a restricted palette of two blues, two yellows, one red, one brown and white.

Sunlight Effect Under the Poplars, 1887, oil on canvas, Staatsgalerie Stuttgart, Germany, 74.3 x 93cm (29 x 37in)

A warm summer afternoon, the sunlight shimmering across a meadow is built up with broken, vibrating layers of small, tick-like brushstrokes. During this period, Monet was particularly intent on capturing the fresh appearance of light and air and spent a great deal of time painting in his local area. The figure in the centre of the canvas is offset by the three tall poplars to the side. The young woman is Suzanne Hoschedé, who is carrying the green parasol she holds in the two large paintings that Monet painted during the previous year.

SERIES AND LATE PAINTINGS

Monet had already made several paintings of the same motif – from haystacks, to tulips, to cliffs and the sea or parts of rivers. But until 1889, he had never painted in such considered succession. The idea was not new to him, it was still about capturing the same motif during different light, weather conditions and seasons – only now he was consciously experimenting. While the cathedral and haystacks series concentrated more on weather effects, his architectural motifs in Venice of canals and palaces emphasized light, water and reflections. His crowning achievement was the work he did at Giverny on his series of water lilies and Japanese bridges. The paintings in this chapter are organized in approximate chronological order, as the series were further developed over the years.

Above: Water Lilies, Morning,
c.1914–18. *From a series of eight large
canvases, entitled* The Water Lilies.
Left: Bright Morning with Willow Trees,
c.1914–18. *From* The Water Lilies.

The Bridge at Vervy, 1889, oil on canvas, Musée Marmottan, Paris, France, 65 x 92cm (26 x 36in)

The poet Maurice Rollinat invited many friends and artists to his home in Creuse, to the south of Paris. In 1889, Geffroy took Monet with him when he went to stay there. Monet set to work immediately, writing to Berthe Morisot: "As you see, here I am again in the back of beyond and getting to grips with the difficulties of a new part of the country."

View of the River Creuse on a Cloudy Day, 1889, oil on canvas, Van der Heydt Museum, Wuppertal, Germany, 73.5 x 92.5cm (29 x 36in)

Having painted the other extreme in Antibes, by 1889 Monet was ready once more to paint nature in all its wildness. "It is superb here, with a terrible wildness that reminds me of Belle Île," he continued in his letter to Berthe Morisot. This work shows his fascination for the effects of light and weather on the scenery. Painted rapidly so he could start another canvas, this incorporates soft, rich colours, despite the overcast weather.

Ravines of the Creuse at the End of the Day, 1889, oil on canvas, Musée Saint-Denis, Reims, France, 65 x 81cm (26 x 32in)

At Fresselines to the south-east of Limoges, Monet painted nine views of the valley at the confluence of the large and small Creuse rivers. Without changing his viewpoint, he altered the colours and brushmarks to describe the play of light and weather effects on the scene. This was painted just before sunset as the sun sank low, throwing dark shadows up the side of the cliffs.

The Creuse Valley Evening Effect, 1889, oil on canvas, Musée Marmottan, Paris, France, 65 x 81cm (26 x 32in)

Monet enthused about the rugged landscape in the valley of the Creuse and as he often did, stayed longer than he had originally intended. This painting is darker than his usual works and the slab-like brushstrokes are thickly layered, creating a heavier and more sombre image than was customary for him. The evening is drawing in and his dark palette, tinged with violet and navy, emphasizes the heavy waters and ravine-like slopes of the valley.

Boating on the Epte, c.1890, oil on canvas, Museu de Arte, São Paulo, Brazil, 133 x 145cm (52 x 57in)

Blanche and Suzanne Hoschedé row along the River Epte, clearly enjoying their outing. Like *The Boat* of 1887, Monet has taken up most of this canvas with delicate ripples of water and foliage. This calm backwater of the Seine was the site of many happy family outings and Monet's speedy response demonstrates the unity and affection within the Monet and Hoschedé families. This picture is just one of many works that Monet painted at the river, and is a precursor to the many water scenes of his pond at Giverny.

The Three Trees, Autumn, 1891, oil on canvas, Private Collection, 92.3 x 73cm (36 x 29in)

Because of Monet's low vantage point, the tops of the closest trees cannot be seen, but disappear off the top of the canvases. He adhered to his philosophy of painting only what he saw, without including any subjective interpretation. He believed that the first clear look at an object was the most honest and the only way in which he could genuinely render atmospheric effects.

Poplars on the Banks of the Epte, c.1891, oil on canvas, Private Collection, 101 x 66cm (40 x 26in)

The years 1890 and 1891 were particularly significant and eventful for Monet, when he was painting his series of poplars. In 1890, he managed to purchase the house and garden at Giverny and he accumulated almost 20,000 francs to buy his late friend Manet's painting *Olympia* from Manet's widow. He decided to donate Manet's work to the nation. Then in 1891, Ernest Hoschedé died, leaving Monet free to marry Alice.

Poplars (or The Four Trees), 1891, oil on canvas, Metropolitan Museum of Art, New York, USA, 81.9 x 81.6cm (32 x 32in)

Having explored different landscapes, by the 1890s, the landscape close to Monet's home captured his attention. He painted the poplars during the summer and autumn of 1891, from his studio boat, which is why they seem to tower up from a low viewpoint and the vertical lines of their slender trunks are emphasized.

Haystacks: Snow Effect, 1891, oil on canvas, National Gallery of Scotland, Edinburgh, Scotland, 65 x 92cm (26 x 36in)

Using the complementary colours of orange and blue to depict the shadows, these haystacks in the snow are vividly painted. Unlike many of his earlier winter paintings, Monet has used astonishingly bright paints to highlight the cold whiteness of the snow. Haystacks have usually long gone by the winter, but Monet persuaded the local farmer to leave them for the autumn and winter of 1890 so that he could paint them.

Haystacks in the Sun, Morning Effect, 1891, oil on canvas, Private Collection, 65 x 100.5cm (26 x 40in)

Monet produced more than 30 paintings of the haystacks, combining work out of doors with some in the studio. Their compact, solid shapes were perfect for him to capture the effects of light but to the contemporary viewer, they were not only an unimaginative subject, but also completely unsuitable for a painting.

Haystack, Hazy Sunshine, 1891, oil on canvas, Private Collection, 60 x 100.5cm (24 x 40in)

Despite their incongruity as a subject, when he exhibited 15 of his Haystacks at Durand-Ruel's gallery in May 1891, the response was sensational. It was Monet's most successful exhibition to date and every painting was sold within three days.

Haystacks at Giverny, 1893, oil on canvas, Private Collection 67 x 100cm (26 x 39in)

Created with several horizontal bands, with the haystack in the centre of the canvas, this image is both rhythmical and lyrical. Gold, green and blue are the dominating colours, created with layers of soft, almost patchy brushmarks. Deep shadows help to pull the painting together. Monet did not follow a structured chronological time span when he changed canvases; it was a more spontaneous capturing of the light.

Haystack at Sunset, 1891, oil on canvas, Boston Museum of Fine Art, Boston, Massachusetts, USA, 73.3 x 92.7cm (29 x 36in)

Monet later declared that the origin of the Haystacks series was the fast changes in atmospheric conditions. As the light changed, he called to Blanche to fetch him another canvas. Each canvas is entirely different from the others: some are vibrant, lyrical, almost abstract, while others are cool, subtle and unassuming. Through his handling, each takes on an almost abstract air.

Rouen Cathedral, 1891,
oil on canvas, Private
Collection, 100 x 65cm
(39 x 26in)

Monet's series paintings can
really be seen as a logical
extension to the
Impressionist principle of
painting the light and
capturing a fleeting moment
in time. He took this one
step further with these
series paintings, in only
painting at a certain time on
a particular canvas. By
changing canvases quickly, he
moved from one passing
moment to another without
being tempted to change
the colours or overwork
a painting.

*Rouen Cathedral, Symphony in
Grey and Rose*, 1892–94, oil
on canvas, National
Museum and Gallery
of Wales, Cardiff, UK,
100 x 65cm (39 x 26in)

Using colour rather than
contour, Monet painted
more than 30 views of the
cathedral in February 1892,
returning the following year
and completing the works at
Giverny between 1893 and
1894. His brushmarks
and colours describe both
the surface detail of the
façade and the sense of
solidity. In May 1895,
Durand-Ruel exhibited 50
paintings, including many
of the Rouen paintings.
As with the Haystacks
series, the critical response
was ecstatic.

Rouen Cathedral, The West Portal, Dull Weather, 1894, oil on canvas, Musée d'Orsay, Paris, France, 100 x 65cm (39 x 26in)

Monet's Cathedrals series is a spectacular demonstration of his determination to capture a particular instant. He did not study the Gothic architecture for itself, but as a base for his artistic explorations. In order to see the changing shapes in different light and weather effects, he purposefully selected a solid, complex object. "Everything changes, even stone," he declared. He applied the paint thickly and vigorously, catching both the rough texture of the cathedral's surface and the vibrations of light – even in overcast, dull weather as in this work. "How hard it is, but it works," he wrote to Alice.

Rouen Cathedral, Foggy Weather, 1894 oil on canvas, Private Collection, 106 x 72.5cm (42 x 29in)

Monet's mood swings once again plagued him during his work on this series of paintings. "Hard as I work, I am not getting anywhere," he wrote to Alice at the end of three weeks' hard work. "Heavens, they really don't know much, the people who think me a master: great intentions, but that's all." It took him another fortnight of constant work to become more reconciled to his efforts. He wrote again to Alice: "Now I am beginning to understand my subject."

The Portal and The Tour d'Albane in the Sunlight, 1893, oil on canvas, Musée d'Orsay, Paris, France, 107 x 73cm (42 x 29in)

The 1890s were a decade of nationalist revival in France and Monet's choice of a French Gothic cathedral in the city where Joan of Arc was martyred could be taken as a patriotic choice. On the other hand, in about 1832, Turner also painted Rouen Cathedral from an almost identical angle, so it might be that Monet was trying out something that another artist had previously painted.

The Portal, 1893, oil on canvas, Pushkin Museum, Moscow, Russia, 100 x 65cm (39 x 26in)

Monet's approach to recording a series became more systematic when he painted Rouen Cathedral. More aware of changing light and weather, he completely changed his palette for each rendering of the façade. To portray the texture of the stone, he created a rough appearance of lights and darks. As he wrote to Alice: "Each day I add something and see something I had not seen before."

The Portal (Harmony in Blue), 1893, oil on canvas, Musée d'Orsay, Paris, France, 91 x 63cm (36 x 25in)

Considering he was only painting from two viewpoints for this series (one was from the window of a nearby house), the range of colours and finishes Monet attained is extremely broad and varied. He was not looking to represent the Gothic architecture for itself, but used it as a support for his artistic vision, enhancing the dark and light tones in a variety of colour ranges in order to emphasize the visual effects he was attempting to achieve.

The Portal, Harmony in Brown, 1892, oil on canvas, Musée d'Orsay, Paris, France, 107 x 73cm (42 x 29in)

With no black in his palette and applying impasto brushstrokes in a variety of tertiary colours, Monet created the appearance of evening light, when the sun had started to sink and the walls were left without golden, pale or even pinkish highlights. Layering light over dark and thicker paint over thin, in the traditional manner of oil painting, this work seems solid and monumental, while it is also hazy and soft.

The Seine at Port-Villez, Evening Effect, 1894, oil on canvas, Musée Marmottan, Paris, France, 52 x 92cm (20 x 36in)

By the 1890s, Monet's colour and texture range was extremely broad despite his use of a fairly reduced palette. Creating a large number of colours from just a few base pigments, this image is soft and diffused, light against dark, pink against grey. In contrast to his small, agitated brushmarks, these smooth, long strokes blend and disperse into each other across the canvas.

Church at Vernon, 1894, oil on canvas, Brooklyn Museum of Art, New York, USA, 65.7 x 92.7cm (26 x 36in)

In 1894, recalling a view he had painted 11 years before, Monet crossed the fields of Giverny to paint the church at Vernon. Using his new method, he painted this view of Vernon six times and, like the Rouen Cathedrals, each canvas gives almost a snapshot of one moment, with particular light, colour and atmosphere.

The Seine at Port-Villez, 1894, oil on canvas, Musée des Beaux-Arts, Rouen, France, 65 x 100cm (26 x 39in)

Monet worked from his studio boat for this series of paintings, painting rapidly as the light effects changed. He continued working on them in his studio, adding final touches to augment the effects he was aiming to render. Eliminating details from the scene, he concentrated on capturing the silvery light and misty atmosphere. Three years previously, he had said: "For me, it is only the surrounding atmosphere which gives subjects their true value."

Cliffs at Varengeville, 1897, oil on canvas, Musée des Beaux-Arts, Le Havre, France, 65 x 92cm (26 x 36in)

From mid-February to April 1896, Monet returned to paint in Pourville and Varengeville and went back there again in January of 1897. In 1896 he produced about 20 paintings there, and in 1897 he painted about 30 canvases of the sea and cliffs. The customs house at Varengeville seems to have been one of his main features. This work is particularly vibrant and energetic.

Waterloo Bridge in Fog,
1899–1901, oil on canvas,
Museum of Fine Arts,
Moscow, Russia,
65 x 100cm (26 x 39in)

During his six-week trip to
London from September
1899, Monet painted this
view of Waterloo Bridge
enveloped in fog. It was
one of many paintings he
created of three different
views of the River Thames.

*Waterloo Bridge, c.*1899,
pastel on paper mounted on
board, Private Collection,
29.2 x 46.4cm (11 x 18in)

Although Monet denied his
talents as a draughtsman, the
drawings and pastels he
produced show his
proficiency. His pastel
drawings for his London
series, produced between
1899 and 1901, are
confident and precise. This
work demonstrates the
importance he put on
drawing as an inherent part
of his work.

Water Lily Pond, 1899, oil on
canvas, Private Collection,
89.5 x 91.5cm (35x 36in)

Monet's Japanese bridge and
water garden was the
culmination of years of
fascination for Japanese
culture and design. In this
work, he placed the horizon
line in the centre of the
canvas and the bridge above
so that viewers rest their
gaze on the surface of the
water where he painted lilies
and other plants.

Water Lily Pond,
1899, oil on canvas,
Philadelphia Museum of
Art, Philadelphia, PA, USA,
89.2 x 93.3cm (35 x 37in)

The water lilies lie on the
surface of the pond like a
patterned, textured carpet.
Only small areas of water
are on view to capture the
reflections of the trees.

Without including too
much detail, Monet has
created the illusion of
perspective – these
flowers seem to recede
into the distance under

the willows. Monet called
these works "water
landscapes" and this
composition derived from
a Japanese print that was
in Monet's collection.

Water Lily Pond: Pink Harmony, 1900, oil on canvas, Musée d'Orsay, Paris, France, 89.5 x 100cm (35 x 39in)

Once his garden was established, Monet used it as a source of inspiration. He designed his water garden as a painting and after 1893, when he extended the pond and built the Japanese bridge, he began painting it. This is produced with small, vertical brushstrokes, layered with many controlled, more spattered marks.

Waterloo Bridge, Morning Fog, 1901, oil on canvas, Philadelphia Museum of Art, Pennsylvania, USA, 65.7 x 100.2cm (26 x 39in)

The heavy stone arches of Waterloo Bridge contrasted with the lighter and more angular framework of Charing Cross Bridge, which he painted at the same time during his visits to London at the turn of the 20th century. This painting explores the effects of the pollution-induced smog. With a palette consisting mainly of blues and violets, he captured the effects of the fog that enveloped the buildings and merged with the mists from the river.

Waterloo Bridge, Misty Morning, 1899–1901, oil on canvas, Hamburger Kunsthalle, Hamburg, Germany, 65 x 100cm (26 x 39in)

Concerned that people might think his work was becoming repetitive, Monet took pains to make sure that even his series were executed in different ways. Industrial pollution greatly affected the weather in London and the resulting fog could change the entire character of the English capital.

Charing Cross Bridge: Fog, 1899–1901, oil on canvas, Art Gallery of Ontario, Toronto, Canada, 73 x 92cm (29 x 36in)

Monet made about 100 oil paintings during his visits to London in 1899 and the following two years. This bridge was built in 1863 to carry trains across the river to and from Charing Cross Station. When his boxes of oil paints were delayed at customs, Monet had to use pastels instead, which possibly helped him to develop an even clearer understanding of proportion and space when his paints arrived.

*A Pathway in Monet's Garden,
Giverny*, 1902, oil on canvas,
Kunsthistorisches Museum,
Vienna, Austria, 89 x 92cm
(35 x 36in)

Monet's garden was the
centre of his world. This side
of it was based on French
and English country gardens,
planted to bloom in the
colours and proportions he
wanted to paint. Every
flower-bed created specific
effects of colour such as this
garden path bordered with
purple irises. At the end
of the path is his pink and
green-shuttered house.

The Houses of Parliament,
1900–01, oil on canvas,
Brooklyn Museum of Art,
New York, USA,
81 x 92cm (32 x 36in)

Monet used colour with an
increasing freedom in his
later years. He looked for
moments when the buildings
appeared in a haze or soft
focus, such as in the dawn,
sunset or evening. Here, the
building is not important, but
is overshadowed by the
atmospheric effect he was
aiming for.

Charing Cross Bridge,
1899–1901, oil on canvas,
Private Collection,
73 x 100cm (29 x 39in)

This view, with its misty
atmosphere and the hint
of boats on the water,
evokes the approach Monet
took in some of his earlier
works such as *Impression,
Sunrise* and *Sunset over
Lavacourt*. With dashing
marks and a mix of pink,
yellow, gold and apricot, the
effect of the sun breaking
through the clouds is
powerful and convincing.

*The Houses of Parliament,
Stormy Sky*, 1900–01, oil on
canvas, Musée des Beaux-
Arts, Lille, France,
81.5 x 92cm (32 x 36in)

Monet's daily letters to
Alice from London show
his obsession with weather
and light effects that
changed almost too
rapidly for him to capture.

He rose at 6 a.m., catching
the clarity of the air
over the Thames and by
9 a.m., when kitchen fires
were lit, smoke created the
fog and he worked again.

Despite his enthusiasm
for all things English,
Monet took the canvases
back to Giverny and
completed them in
the studio.

Houses of Parliament, Sunset,
1900–01, oil on canvas,
Kunsthaus Zürich, Zurich,
Switzerland,
81 x 92cm (32 x 36in)

Discernible brushstrokes
build up this spectacular
interplay of light using
dramatic colour and bright
contrasts. Colours involved
are mainly the three
primaries, and the painting
recalls *The Burning of the
Houses of Parliament* painted
by Turner in 1834. Monet
continued working on these
canvases for years, skilfully
maintaining the spontaneous
appearance of shimmering
colours in this backlit work.

Parliament, Reflections on the Thames, 1900–1, oil on canvas, Musée Marmottan, Paris, France, 81 x 92cm (32 x 36in)

In capturing the sparkling effects of sunlight forcing its rays through the clouds to highlight the ripples on the river, Monet was sure of which colours and brushstrokes to use. In actual fact, he was not as confident as the final paintings seem to imply. When he was working on these works back in Giverny, he would not sell even the completed canvases as he said he needed them all so he could complete the rest.

Nympheas, 1907, oil on canvas, Private Collection, 100.3 x 100.3cm (39 x 39in)

By eliminating horizon lines, Monet took a bold step and concentrated solely on looking down on to his pond.

Logically and in hindsight, this seems the obvious step he could have taken, but after so many radical directions, this could have been seen as one step too far. The main features of this work are its vibrant colours and lively brushmarks.

Water Lilies, 1907, oil on canvas, Private Collection, 100 x 73cm (39 x 29in)

Painted as a speedy series of just a few canvases, Monet clearly enjoyed the contrasts of deep and light colours and shapes in this transitory arrangement of light and reflections. Feathery paint marks highlight the sketchiness of the work and give it the (incorrect) impression of being a preparatory pattern of colours rather than a genuine representation of a spontaneous occurrence of nature.

Water Lilies, 1907, oil on canvas, Musée Marmottan, Paris, France, 100 × 73cm (39 × 29in)

By June of 1907, Monet's eyesight had deteriorated. Almost feeling his way, he painted these reflections on his pond with vertical strokes of fairly thin paint to describe the willows, layered with thicker paint over the top to represent the lilies. Colours are still relatively authentic and the result is a lush, peaceful world seen through his unique vision.

Nympheas, 1908, oil on canvas, Private Collection, 92 × 73cm (36 × 29in)

With these canvases, Monet launched a new trend in landscape painting once more. Other artists soon began capturing fugitive effects, using varied and decorative brushstrokes. Here, the features that normally created the illusion of perspective diminished as he focused on the surface of the water, building up deliberately tangled marks in vivid colours. The intricate colours and shapes belie his failing eyesight.

View of Venice, 1908, oil on canvas, Private Collection, 73 × 92cm (29 × 36in)

After his trip to Venice with Alice, Monet completed several canvases in Giverny. Painting in pinks, oranges, purples and blues, he felt that the unique atmosphere of Venice was beyond his power to capture and that he could not do it justice. It was not until 1912 that he was willing to release 29 of his Venetian canvases for an exhibition.

Palazzo Dario, 1908, oil on canvas, National Museum and Gallery of Wales, Cardiff, Wales, UK, 92.3 x 73.2cm (36 x 29in)

Monet's Venetian paintings were all reworked back in his studio in Giverny, far more than most of his other works, which were usually painted from direct observation with minimal adjustments later. Although this method gives the Venetian paintings a multi-layered, multicoloured appearance, Monet felt he could not remember the distinctive atmosphere and later remarked: "It is detestable…I finished from memory and nature has had her revenge."

Venice: Rio de Santa Salute, 1908, oil on canvas, Private Collection, 81.3 x 64.8cm (32 x 25in)

It was in autumn 1908 that Monet and Alice went to Venice, so there was some bad weather. It rained for days and when the sun reappeared, Monet's enthusiasm to paint had diminished. He wrote to Durand-Ruel and other dealers that he would return with just a few sketches or experiments. This painting is one of those; an ephemeral vision of buildings rising out of the water.

Gondola in Venice, 1908, oil on canvas, Musée des Beaux-Arts, Nantes, France, 81 x 55cm (32 x 22in)

On 3 December 1908, Monet made this study, later giving it to his friend Clemenceau without adjusting it or adding anything. It captures the essence of Venice and was painted when they had set their departure date for four days later on 7 December. He and Alice had enjoyed a particularly relaxing holiday and who knew when, if ever, they could return or have a similar break?

Yellow and Purple Irises,
1924–25, oil on canvas,
Musée Marmottan, Paris,
France, 106 x 155cm
(42 x 61in)

Monet did not just paint the surface of his pond during his later years, but also often painted the irises that grew next to it. For this work, he looked through the irises and up to the sky. It is almost a worm's eye view and quite a contrast to some of the aerial scenes he had painted during previous years.

Water Lilies: Morning,
1914–18, oil on canvas,
Musée de l'Orangerie, Paris,
France, 200 x 200cm
(79 x 79in)

At Giverny, Monet began planning his *Grandes Décorations;* water lily paintings for public display, to create a place for meditation, and to reflect on the men who had died for the nation in World War I.

Water Lilies: Green Reflection,
1914, oil on canvas, Musée
de l'Orangerie, Paris,
France, 200 x 425cm
(79 x 167in)
Despite problems with his
sight, Monet's pond was a
constant source of
inspiration and he painted
his canvases of it in a vibrant
and deliberate manner.
Here, his palette included
cobalt, ultramarine, cadmium
yellow, viridian, cadmium
red, zinc white and cobalt
violet. All the colours are
clear; paint is thin in the
underlying layers and thicker
on the top – there is an
enduring sense of vigour.

Clear Morning with Willows, 1920–26, oil on canvas, Musée de l'Orangerie, Paris, France, 200 x 425cm (79 x 167in)

The theme of water lilies first appeared in Monet's work in 1898. He produced more from 1903 to 1909 and then worked on them again from 1914. They became larger over time.

Water Lilies, 1914–17, oil on canvas, Musée Marmottan, Paris, France, 130 x 150cm (51 x 59in)

The paint is so thick in some places and the colours are so pure that Monet probably squeezed some of it straight out of the tube on to his canvas. No longer a painter of horizons, skies and land, Monet now included sky only as reflections of clouds scudding across the water's surface. The water here is painted almost transparently, with the lilies painted in more opaque paint.

Water Lilies: Morning, 1920–26, oil on canvas, Musée de l'Orangerie, Paris, France, 200 x 212.5cm (79 x 84in)

Delayed by his health problems, Monet's huge water lily paintings took several years to complete. It was a difficult time for him, although Blanche was his constant assistant. Despite dips into depression, however, he still managed to produce these ethereal works; with soft, misty reflections and ripples and light and colour on the surface of the water.

Water Lilies: Harmony in Blue, 1914–17, oil on canvas, Musée Marmottan, Paris, France, 200 x 200cm (79 x 79in)

From 1897 until his death in 1926, Monet constantly painted his water lilies. He wrote: "These landscapes of water and reflection have become an obsession. It is beyond my strength as an old man, yet I want to succeed in conveying what I feel." In this canvas, the blue, green, pink and lilac hues predominate as he aimed to reproduce the natural phenomena he experienced in his own private world.

Detail of Water Lilies: Clouds, 1920–26, oil on canvas, Musée de l'Orangerie, Paris, France, 200 x 425cm (79 x 167in)

This painting is created with darker initial layers and lighter colours on top. He added vibrancy with the Venetian technique of layering cool colours over a warm covering.

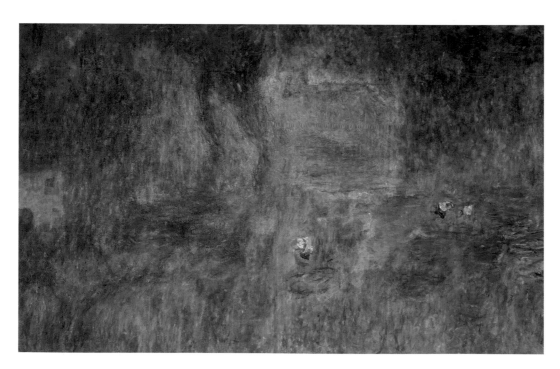

Water Lilies: Reflections of Trees, 1920–26, central section, oil on canvas, Musée de l'Orangerie, Paris, France, 200 x 425cm (79 x 167in)

Proust wrote about these works: "Flowers of the earth, yet also flowers of the water, these tender water lilies which the Master has depicted in sublime paintings including this garden…are like a first, living sketch." Each of the canvases were immersed in colour, particularly in shades of blue, with mere hints of shapes and forms around the pond.

SERIES AND LATE PAINTINGS 241

Nympheas, 1916–19, oil on canvas, Private Collection, 200 x 180cm (79 x 71in)

In 1917 and 1919 respectively, Degas and Renoir died; the last of Monet's original artist friends. Although he still had Michel and his stepchildren as well as several other friends, he immersed himself in a rhythm of work, painting intensely, as if he felt that his work was crucial now that his friends could no longer help him to lead the way.

Weeping Willow and the Water Lily Pond, 1916–19, oil on canvas, Musée Marmottan, Paris, France, 200 x 180cm (79 x 71in)

The first layers of these works are almost transparent, but they can be seen through the more vigorous brushwork and impasto layers.

His brushstrokes range from abbreviated, short flicks to longer, more fluid marks. With his eye problems, his colours moved from authentic imitations of nature, to more audacious, unexpected hues, influencing many younger artists and art movements of the 20th century.

Water Lilies, 1916–19, oil on canvas, Musée Marmottan, Paris, France, 200 x 180cm (79 x 71in)

Often disheartened, sometimes angry with the results of his efforts, Monet still continued to destroy paintings that he was not happy with. This work is one of more than 200 on the subject of his water lilies where Monet continued to disregard perspective, to create the pond surface out of vertical marks and the lily pads with sweeping, horizontal brushstrokes and broken dashes of lighter highlights.

Nympheas, 1916–19, oil on canvas, Musée Marmottan, Paris, France, 200 x 180cm (79 x 71in)

Painting from the water's edge, the focus of this work is the willow fronds. The paint was applied thinly and rapidly, using mainly yellow ochre, French ultramarine, cobalt blue and cobalt violet.

As he aged, Monet's obsession with his work did not decline and he continued working long hours every day even though all around him was bleak. In the midst of World War I, his stepson was conscripted, his friend Clemenceau's son had been wounded and Renoir's son was shot.

Self-Portrait, 1917, oil on canvas, Musée d'Orsay, Paris, France, 70 x 55cm (28 x 22in)

One of Monet's rare self-portraits, this was painted when he was concentrating on his lily paintings. It was the year of his brother Léon's death and although outwardly he did not appear to have been as close to his brother as he once was, perhaps this expressive portrait was a reaction; a way of searching into his genetic make-up and remembering his sibling.

*The Lily Pond, c.*1917, oil on canvas, Private Collection, 98 × 130.5cm (39 × 51in)

After the deaths of Alice in 1911 and of his son Jean in 1914, Monet became more withdrawn and reclusive. His lifelong interest in Japanese art is apparent in all his compositions and, despite his 77 years, his willingness to experiment continued to increase. Many other younger artists were moving in new directions, but Monet, tucked away in his Giverny studio, continued to break new ground.

Water Lilies, 1917–20, oil on canvas, Musée Marmottan, Paris, France, 100 × 300cm (39 × 118in)

The lilies form a continuous pattern across the surface of the canvas. To the end of his life, Monet continued trying to catch the ephemeral appearance of his pond as light and weather conditions altered. Here, through the hastiest of scrubs of unmixed paint, with no underpainting and an absence of his familiar colours, he has rendered the moment when misty air mingles with the pond water.

Yellow and Lilac Water Lilies, 1914–17, oil on canvas, The Toledo Museum of Art, Toledo, Ohio, USA, 200 x 215cm (79 x 85in)

The *Grandes Décorations* (the vast panels featuring the water lily pond) preoccupied Monet for five years before he gave them to the French nation at the end of World War I. They continued to dominate his output for years after. He never became bored with them because there were too many effects and sensations to capture. Here, a bright midday sun causes the reflections to change from blue to green to lavender.

The Japanese Bridge, 1918–24, oil on canvas, Musée Marmottan, Paris, France, 89 x 116cm (35 x 46in)

Monet's Japanese Bridge paintings took several years to create. He worked on them during the summer and autumn after lunch on days when the heat in his studio was too overpowering. The strong and strange colours, distorted shapes and shaky lines show how difficult it was for him to see clearly and in January 1923, he had four cataract operations. In 1924, he resumed painting these works, continuing to layer thick paint on to his canvases.

The Japanese Bridge at Giverny, 1918–24, oil on canvas, Musée Marmottan, Paris, France, 89 x 116cm (35 x 46in)

Understandably terrified of the blindness that seemed to be descending upon him, Monet was determined to paint as much as he could before his eyes completely failed. He often began these works, set them aside and worked on them repeatedly much later. This was one of those that he said were really about five works in one. The paint texture has built up so thickly that it is almost in relief.

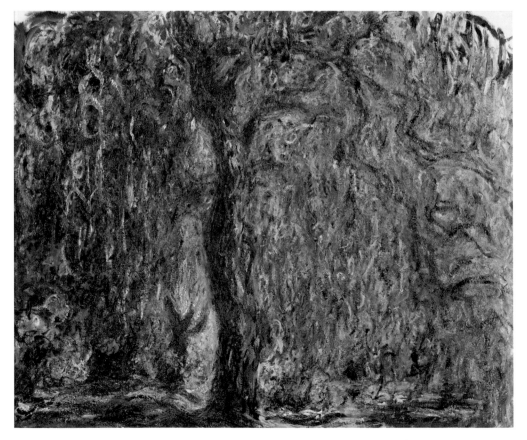

Weeping Willow, 1918–19, oil on canvas, Musée Marmottan, Paris, France, 100 x 120cm (39 x 47in)

Moving away from the overhead view of his pond, Monet occasionally painted his weeping willow trees. Painted on an easel and taking a more normal viewpoint, he applied several layers of wriggling, waving brushstrokes in bold, bright colours. Viewers look through a dense amount of leafy fronds and tendrils to further vegetation. Light barely filters through the leaves and branches, but where it does, it practically sparkles.

The Yellow Irises, c.1918–25,
oil on canvas,
Private Collection,
56 x 48cm (22 x 19in)

While painting his large pond and bridge paintings, Monet occasionally rendered some of the flowers from his garden separately. He devoted several canvases to flowers on blue backgrounds, simply rendered and in impasto paint. These works are entirely different from his earlier flower paintings, such as *Chrysanthemums* of 1878 and 1882, with few details and a more liberated approach.

The Japanese Bridge, 1918,
oil on canvas, Musée
Marmottan, Paris, France,
100 x 200cm (39 x 79in)

With a cataract in one eye and a disease in the other, Monet eventually overcame his anxieties and had three successive operations on his right eye. His surgeon was satisfied, but Monet was less so. Yellow constantly coloured everything he saw and while he was waiting for special lenses to counteract the problem, many of his works have a noticeable predominance of yellow hues.

Weeping Willow, 1918–19, oil on canvas, Musée Marmottan, Paris, France, 100 x 110cm (39 x 43in)

Monet's plan to paint his pond had originally been conceived years earlier. He said: "The temptation came to me to use this water lily theme for the decoration of a drawing room….Along the walls, enveloping all the partitions…it would have produced the illusion of an endless whole…with no horizon and no shore; nerves exhausted by work would have relaxed there…[It] would have offered a refuge of peaceful meditation."

Water Lilies, 1914–17, oil on canvas, Private Collection, 200 x 200cm (79 x 79in)

In order to create a place for meditation and to reflect on the young men who had given their lives for the nation in World War I, Monet's sense of mission was integral to his aim, which was to produce many panels called *Nympheas* (water lilies), which he wanted to donate to the nation. Uncomfortable with the contrast between his life painting his lily pond and the young men fighting at the Front, he tried to stop thinking of it and immersed himself in textures of his lilies and the water beneath them.

The Japanese Bridge at Giverny, 1918–24, oil on canvas, Musée Marmottan, Paris, France, 89 x 100cm (35 x 39in)

Eventually Monet realized that by painting, he was upholding some of the beauty and some of the spirit of France. Each time an enemy invasion threatened, he refused to leave Giverny, insisting that he would rather die among his beloved paintings. Going beyond the original doctrines of Impressionism, he worked harder and more intensely in trying to recreate what he saw on to canvas.

The Japanese Bridge, 1918–24, oil on canvas, Musée Marmottan, Paris, France, 74 x 92cm (29 x 36in)

Tightly focusing on the Japanese bridge as he had so many times, Monet created a closely framed composition with neither foreground nor background. At the age of 78, he said: "My life is spent thinking only of what I am doing, my confounded painting. When evening comes I ponder and think only of what I have done in the day, looking forward to the next day, with the hope of doing better."

Weeping Willows, the Water Lily Pond at Giverny, 1916–19, oil on canvas, Private Collection, 150 × 131cm (59 × 52in)

Monet worked in his newly built studio, specially designed and constructed in 1915, despite the ravages and privations of World War I. While he could work on the largest canvases indoors in the studio all year round, the smaller pictures like this would either be placed on an easel or held up with an arrangement of ropes and weights so that he could paint in front of the pond itself.

Wisteria (Glycines), c.1919–20, oil on canvas, Allen Memorial Art Museum, Oberlin College, Ohio, USA, 149.8 × 200.5cm (59 × 79in)

This was one of nine paintings originally intended to be part of a continuous decorative frieze that would be placed above the water lily murals. Although the plan never came to fruition, nine canvases of wisteria still remain. In this study of wisteria, Monet depicts a garland with heavy, looping flowers. The predominant colours are ultramarine and cobalt blue.

The Large Willow at Giverny, 1918, oil on canvas, Private Collection, 130 x 110cm (51 x 43in)

As a consequence of impaired eyesight, Monet painted this primarily in turquoise and yellow, with an almost frenzied application of brushmarks. The bold, almost abstracted brushwork that characterized all his works at the time is equally evident here as in his larger canvases of this time. In vigorous strokes, sometimes with the thickness of impasto, he created a cascade of colour.

Wisteria, 1919, oil on canvas, Musée Marmottan, Paris, France, 100 x 300cm (39 x 118in)

On the Japanese bridge, Monet had an arch built and planted wisteria plants to climb up it and to hang down in bunches, which he loved when they had grown sufficiently to touch the surface of the water, so they and their reflections became one. This canvas was created as a commission for the pavilion in the garden of the Hotel Biron, but the project was abandoned in 1921.

Water Lily Pond, 1917–19, oil on canvas, Private Collection, 100 x 200cm (39 x 79in)

Monet's water lily paintings were on a scale that had never been contemplated before for paintings of flowers. The word 'décoratif' was used with these works because of their modern and abstracted appearance.

Wisteria, 1919–20, oil on canvas, Haags Gemeentemuseum, The Hague, Netherlands, 150.5 x 200cm (59 x 79in)

Monet produced several canvases of his wisteria, revelling in rendering their delicate fragility. Although the paintings seem sketchy and incomplete, they were completely finished. In 1923, he had an eye operation, which meant that bluer shades appear more often in his paintings.

Water Lilies, c.1920–26, oil on canvas, Chrysler Museum, Norfolk, Virginia, USA (Dimensions unknown)

In 1918, one of Monet's friends described his studio: "…a dozen canvases placed one after another in a circle on the ground, all about six feet wide by four feet high: a panorama of water and water lilies, of light and sky." Intended as part of his series for the nation, they were not included, and remained in his studio after his death.

The Artist's House from the Rose Garden, 1922–24, oil on canvas, Musée Marmottan, Paris, France, 81 x 93cm (32 x 37in))

Even in old age, Monet painted with passion. "A colour will appear again which I'd seen and daubed on one of these canvases the day before. Quickly the picture is brought over to me, and I do my utmost to fix the vision definitively, but it generally disappears as fast as it arose, giving way to a different colour already tried several days before on another study, which at once is set before me – and so it goes the whole day!"

The Roses, 1925–26, oil on canvas, Musée Marmottan, Paris, France, 130 x 200cm (51 x 79in)

In 1923, Monet's sight was restored after an operation and his enthusiasm was as strong as ever. His skill and ideas had never lessened and his paintings continued to surprise and influence the wider art world. With relatively few brushstrokes, he created these gently blooming roses. Seeming to float against a blue summer sky, his roses reflect the summer light. The painting is calm and serene but also full of energy.

INDEX

Below: Camille on the Beach at Trouville, 1870.

Above: Small Fishing Boats at Pourville, *1882.*